I Bet You Won't Read This
(Confessions of a Night Time Radio Host)

Ian Collins

THE CUTS

INTRODUCTION BY IAN COLLINS

CHAPTER 1
Meet the Creatures

CHAPTER 2
Talky Bits

CHAPTER 3
Who Calls?

CHAPTER 4
The Lists

CHAPTER 5
Ian's Untold Story

CHAPTER 6
The Gallery

CHAPTER 7
Poignant Moments

CHAPTER 8
The Hate Mail

CHAPTER 9
How to get into Radio

You will notice that this book contains no page numbers – different eh? We're not having you lot just flicking through and searching out ya favourite bits, you're gonna read the whole damn thing.

A publication by
The Radio Book

This paperback edition 2000

First published in Great Britain by
The Radio Book 2000

Copyright © Ian Collins 2000

Printed in Great Britain by
Leiston Press
Unit 1B
Masterlord Industrial Park
Leiston, Suffolk
IP16 4XS

All rights reserved. No part of this publication may be reproduced, stored in a retrieval system, or transmitted, in any form or by any means, electronic, mechanical, photocopying, recording or otherwise, without prior permission of the publishers.

This book is sold subject to the condition that it shall not, by way of trade or otherwise, be lent, re-sold, hired out or otherwise circulated without the publishers prior consent in any form of binding or cover other than that in which it is published and without a similar condition including this condition being imposed on the subsequent purchaser.

WWW.THERADIOBOOK.COM

Illustrations for
Children
&
Adults.

Douglas J Pledger

Contact BT Artists. (www.btartists.com),
dougpledger@yahoo.com

Copyright D.Pledger/Bernard Thornton Artists

If someone had told me ten years ago that by the year 2000 I would be the only national night-time phone-in host in the UK, I would have thought they'd just arrived from the land of the fabled banana. As we sit here today, this statement is indeed true. Before the pedantic brigade start sounding off, let me clear something up here. I define nights as in 'through the night'; and in the use of the word 'only' I refer to the fact that I do this full time, as opposed to colleagues whose sterling work takes place on the weekends (Believe me, having worked for almost ten years in phone and speech based formats, it's important to clear these things up. One word out of place and some goon wants to fry you from the inside out). It is perhaps a sad reflection on the state of British radio that there is still only one truly interactive national radio station – talkSPORT. This fact might be great news for me and the shareholders but, I believe, it's a pretty sad state of affairs for listener choice.

The initial idea for this book was based on what one might call "Hate Mail" the more nefarious correspondence that I've received in nearly a decade of presenting phone based formats. This still remains the backbone of the book. With that in mind, there are a couple of points worth making now. Firstly, anyone who works in radio presentation is, for some bizarre reason, deemed to be on a pedestal. For the dubious few - and it is a few - you become a kind of target. Words are over-analysed, your personal life becomes of interest and your entire personality is assumed on the basis of a radio show. This is true for Music Jocks as well as Talk Show Hosts. However, in phone-in formats, you become even more magnified: the crutch of music is gone, the swift ten second patter between songs becomes a continuous four hours of non-stop speech, and you, not the records, take centre stage.

The finer details of those who choose to write 'colourful' letters is covered in the Hate Mail chapter. Therefore, all I would say at this stage is that receiving a bit of twisted correspondence is, I believe, simply par for the course in this industry, a kind of occupational hazard. I'm not a Shock Jock and I've never set out to offend and so I have to assume that being on the receiving end of strange packages and imaginative words (which incidentally form a mere 0.1% of the post bag) simply goes with the territory. The extremes of this kind of behaviour are highlighted in films such as *Play Misty for Me* and *Talk Radio*. Thankfully, nothing has ever gone quite that far. Of all the media, radio is by far the most intimate. As distinct from TV - where the big box in the corner often becomes background entertainment - radio, particularly late night radio, seems to go straight to the very centre of the mind. A single word, a phrase, a change of intonation or an emphasis on a particular sentence is all that's required for some odd bod to decide that your entire personality is questionable, your job should be taken from you and ideally you should be strung up by the fundaments and left to stew in the sewers of Satan's pantry.

Anyway, enough of this idle buffoonery, let's get to the point. Having set out to compile a collection of letters from the Fruit Bats (which should be enough entertainment to last a lifetime) I decided to add the additional element of my radio shows themselves. For those who have followed programmes that I've hosted, this should provide a nice little insight into the background, production teams and inner workings of some of those programmes. If you've never heard me - WHERE THE HELL HAVE YOU BEEN? Either way, I hope this book provides a unique peep into life behind the microphone, as well as some of the escapades in front of it. This book is also designed to be a vital tool for those wanting to enter the radio industry. Not only will it give you an insight into the finer workings of an on-going radio programme, but I've also included a chapter specifically written for those looking for a way in. Few books on radio are written from this angle. I sincerely hope it give you a swift boot in the right direction.

So here's my radio history in brief. As you will have gathered, I'm currently residing at the UK's only dedicated National Sports Talk Station - talkSPORT (1089/1053AM or talksport.net) - hosting *Ian Collins and the Creatures of the night* (Tuesday - Friday 1am - 5am). talkSPORT provides an unrivalled, interactive, sporting output for the majority of the day but continues to diversify into highly original phone-based formats at night. When I was first offered this gig, I was working in regional BBC Radio in Kent, England. I'd recently left the Capital Radio Group where I was hosting an evening phone-in show five nights a week on Invicta FM, again in Kent. When I left Independent Radio to join what was considered the ageing local BBC, most of my colleagues thought I'd gone stark raving mad: I'd been presenting a successful phone based music show, with a large audience, and I was leaving to host the early breakfast programme (5am - 7am - which means rising at 3am) on a station whose listeners appeared to be older than God's dog. However, there was a plan. I needed to move into a full-time speech/news format in order to brush up on what I considered were the necessary skills to make the step to a national station. (Aside from anything else, working at the BEEB enabled me to get my mitts on their mighty contacts files and winkle out a few useful names and numbers - I once rang the PM's home for a dare - he wasn't available). I knew the BBC was never going to be my final home and so I told myself I would only stay there for six months. In the event, I stayed there for six months and six days.

Eventually, as I had hoped, the call came from what was then called Talk Radio – the UK's first national talk station. I was initially offered 5 overnight shows a week starting on April 10th 1995. It was the first time in my life that I can remember quite literally jumping for joy. I accepted. Again, there was some cynicism from colleagues who thought that even the dull early shift in local radio was somehow "better" than the dreaded GRAVEYARD SHIFT on the national airwaves. It's a kind of odd psychology that I still meet from time to time: "Oh no, you do the graveyard shift? That must be terrible". Well, if it was terrible I wouldn't do it, you dinks. If we were talking music radio, then wild horses couldn't drag me to those hours, but phone-in radio, that's a different story. In many ways this kind of format comes into its own during the twilight hours. In the United States, folk would tear your arm off to get hold of a show with those hours – there's nothing taboo about working the Late Shift there.

Anyway kids, that's enough from me, you've got a book to read. Any spelling mistakes or grammatical errors are purely the fault of the proof reader and nothing whatsoever to do with me. If you're offended by bad language or matters sexual then pass this book on pretty damn quick to someone who isn't.

I'm told by author friends that it's procedure to thank folk who assisted, in whatever way, in putting a book together. If I'm honest, there are so many I'd be afraid of missing someone out. With that in mind, big thanks to *all* those special people who have been there at the right times – you know who you are.

Ian Collins – London 2000

Chapter 1.

Meet the Creatures

The format of my programme is unashamedly 'zoo'. That's radio speak meaning that in addition to myself, the team that work alongside me also appear on the air. Over the years that team has changed. As with any line-up things move on, people change jobs and formats evolve.

The original Creature line-up was Mike Hanson, Kev the Wondersheep and myself. When I first met this pair of bozos I nearly packed my bags and went home. Kev wore funny waistcoats and walked in a simian manner and Hanson was way-too Canadian for my liking. However, a series of high-level board meetings and a swift salary hike managed to twist my arm and convince me to stay. It was tough at first and working with them proved taxing. However, we found common ground and pulled it off. The show hit the airwaves like a super-charged rocket and swiftly dented the listening figures of our rivals. That said, I'm still extremely wary of both of them.

Next came the girl Mulvey, a feminist academic who seemed about as compatible with my logic as a yak. I had a sneaky feeling I'd have to train this one with big sticks and vicious animals. She surprised us all. In the first 10 minutes of meeting she made her position clear: she might be female, she might be new, but she was determined to fit in and work as part of the team - nothing was going to faze her. Naturally we ignored her and it was a full 4 weeks before I realised she was still working with me. Over time, things got better and it wasn't long before Sarah and I hit it off. We've since managed to enjoy many a good debate as well as countless coffee nights in Soho Cafes. She still can't beat me at chess though.

It wasn't too much later that a long haired hippie with John Lennon glasses turned up at the studios looking for a bit of work experience. He gave us some cock and bull story about being in a band and wanting a career in radio. He didn't even have a name. We took him on as an occasional phone turkey and trained him up to conform to the Creature code of conduct. That meant the hair had to go, the glasses needed changing and the denim dungarees would be ritually burnt. I also decided, having spent weeks calling him 'you' and 'thing', he should have a name. I called him Miff and just like dog's poop, he stuck. That boy stayed around for about 4 years, on and off.

As with all radio teams, we sometimes need a spare pair of hands. What's the point in paying for someone when a bonehead like Pop-up-Pete turns up on your doorstep with a sorry story about needing a break and a huge lie about his parents disowning him in favour of a Spaniel called Giblet? This kid was one sad sight, but nothing that a good dose of Creature indoctrination wouldn't sort out. The boy worked his nuts off and by a creature vote of 2/1, it was decided that he should become a paid member of staff. From being the humble, freebie work experience boy, this guy wound up being our full time technical producer and getting more fan mail than me - the clown. When Pete left to become a psychiatric nurse, the search was on for a suitable replacement. Enter Scott (later to be called Phone-Sex Scott due to his penchant for a telephonic swift one!). This dozy dollop hardly knew what a radio station was before we whipped him under our nocturnal wing. He has an IQ of 6, a personal freshness problem and likes Jean-Claude Van Dam. You get the picture.

So as you can see, over the years I've been blessed with some of life's greatest retards. They seem to follow me. Somehow between this incredible mish-mash of personalities, we've been able to make this damn show work and have dominated the national dial ever since.

Please meet The Creatures of the Night.

MIKE HANSON

Position on the Show: SENIOR PRODUCER

Place of birth: TORONTO, CANADA

Hobbies: GOLF, BASEBALL

Favourite Song: JUMPIN' JACK FLASH - ROLLING STONES

Favourite Film: SPINAL TAP

Favourite Book: THE FLASHMAN NOVELS - GEORGE MACDONALD FRASER

Favourite Quote: 'YOU TALKIN' TO ME?' - ARNIE

Favourite Word: CRYOGENICS

Previous Jobs: DOOR TO DOOR COOKBOOK SALESMAN, PETROL PUMP ATTENDANT

Current Job: PROGRAMME MANAGER, TALKSPORT

CREATURE FACT
Ian first set foot in a radio studio at the BBC! He was 14 when he wrote to Gloria Hunniford and asked to sit in on her show. The producer called him up and invited him in. Ian says Gloria was lovely but the studios were scary – at the time the BBC had a policy of unisex toilets. Peeing next to Glo just ain't right, he said.

KEV THE WONDERSHEEP

Position on the Show: CO-PRODUCER

Place of birth: STIRLING, SCOTLAND

Hobbies: SARCASM, CHEESE, TOMFOOLERY

Favourite Song: RUNNIN' RIOT - COCKSPARRA

Favourite Film: THE INCREDIBLE TWO HEADED TRANSPLANT

Favourite Book: THIS ONE

Favourite Quote: 'WIN IF YOU CAN..IF YOU CAN'T - CHEAT' - ANON.

Favourite Word: PLINTH

Previous Jobs: PLACING MOTORWAY CONES

Current Job: TOP-FLIGHT, HOT-SHOT RADIO PRODUCER

CREATURE FACT
Miff once shared a bath with superstar football boy Bobby Moore.
He was a nipper at the time and became a team mascot for a match.
He said that Bobby was the perfect gentleman who not only gave him a few good football tips but also introduced him to some colourful changing room terminology.

SARAH MULVEY

Position on the Show: CO-PRODUCER

Place of birth: SUSSEX, ENGLAND

Hobbies: LEARNING TO DRIVE, BABY SITTING GODSON ALEX

Favourite Song: 'UNTOUCHABLE FACE' - ANI DIFRANCO

Favourite Film: DR ZHIVAGO

Favourite Book: THE OED

Favourite Quote: 'IT'S ONLY A GAME SHOW' - HOUSEMATES, CHANNEL 4'S BIG BROTHER

Favourite Word: FLOCCINAUCCINIHILIPILIFICATION

Previous Jobs: TOILET CLEANER (HER OWN ONLY)

Current Job: FREELANCE TELEVISION DIRECTOR/PRODUCER

CREATURE FACT
The best-selling novelist Fiona Walker listens to the show while penning her mighty shelf breakers. Her books include "Snap Happy", "Between Males" and "Girls' Night In".
(Available in all good book stores!)

MIFF DANIELS

Position on the Show: CO-PRODUCER

Place of birth: LONDON, ENGLAND

Hobbies: DRINKING, GOING TO THE PUB, MORE DRINKING

Favourite Song: ANARCHY IN THE UK - THE SEX PISTOLS

Favourite Film: THE ITALIAN JOB

Favourite Book: THE WASP FACTORY - IAIN BANKS

Favourite Quote: 'REMOVE YOUR PANTS BEFORE RESORTING TO VIOLENCE' - YOKO ONO

Favourite Word: ****** ******

Previous Jobs: PUB LANDLORD, BAND MANAGER, AUCTIONEER

Current Job: FREELANCE TV & RADIO PRESENTER

CREATURE FACT
Kev the Wondersheep used to be Miff's lodger. During his stay, he never cooked, played odd music and never let anyone see inside his boudoir.
That boy is weird.

POP UP PETE

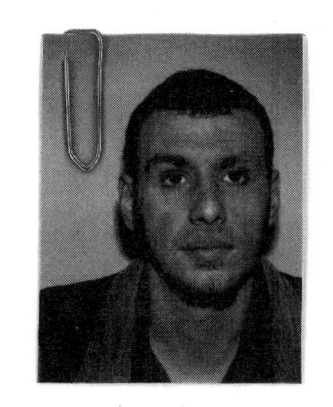

Position on the Show: TECHNICAL PRODUCER

Place of birth: LONDON, ENGLAND

Hobbies: CRICKET, PLAYING WITH FIREWORKS

Favourite Song: MARY'S BOY CHILD - HARRY BELAFONTE

Favourite Film: CASINO

Favourite Book: CLOCKWORK ORANGE - ANTHONY BURGESS

Favourite Quote: 'NO ONE IS PERFECT IN THIS IMPERFECT WORLD' - PATRICE LUMUMBA

Favourite Word: ENAMOURED

Previous Jobs: WORKED IN A CAFÉ

Current Job: RADIO DJ ON ATLANTIC 252

CREATURE FACT

Ian recently traced his family tree. He was astonished to discovery that he's not as English as he first thought. The research revealed that the boy from Lincolnshire is actually part Irish, part Scottish and a dash of Yank.
How do you put that lot on ya passport?

PHONE-SEX SCOTT

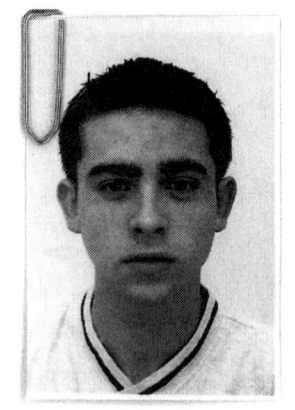

Position on the Show: TECHNICAL PRODUCER

Place of birth: LONDON, ENGLAND

Hobbies: GOLF, PLAYING WITH ANYTHING TECHNICAL

Favourite Song: THE ONLY WAY IS UP - YAZZ

Favourite Film: ANYTHING WITH JEAN-CLAUDE VAN DAM

Favourite Book: HARRY POTTER SERIES

Favourite Quote: 'ME TARZAN' - TARZAN

Favourite Word: FATHOM

Previous Jobs: 192 BOY FOR BT, PRINTER

Current Job: TECHNICAL PROD. FOR IAN COLLINS

CREATURE FACT
Mike Hanson once saw Elvis Presley live in Toronto when he was 6 years old. His parents took him along to the gig and Mike says he definitely recalls seeing the man in full cat suit regalia. Whether Elvis was munching cheeseburgers and sat on the John at the time is not known.

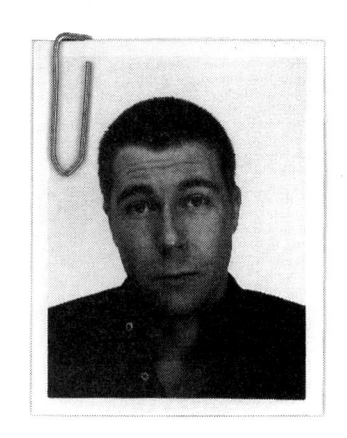

IAN COLLINS

Position on the Show: THE HOST

Place of birth: LINCOLNSHIRE, ENGLAND

Hobbies: CANOEING, RIDING, READING

Favourite Song: MANY RIVERS TO CROSS – JIMMY CLIFF

Favourite Film: CITIZEN KANE

Favourite Book: STRAIT IS THE GATE – ANDRÉ GIDE

Favourite Quote: 'NEVER STOOP SO LOW AS TO HATE ANOTHER MAN' – GEORGE WASHINGTON

Favourite Word: SCENARIO

Previous Jobs: STAGEHAND, BLUECOAT

Current Job: TALK SHOW HOST & WRITER

CREATURE FACT
Sarah has a rather distinct academic background. She attended both Oxford and Cambridge consecutively. During her time at Oxbridge she met an array of prominent folk including Margaret Thatcher, Ronald Reagan and Salman Rushdie. Two out of the three were actually OK, she said.

BONUS CREATURES

Over the years, we've also picked up additional reprobates to the Creature team. Most joined us for work experience and ended up sticking like glue. Some have gone on to full time jobs in the media, others are still in education, many just fell by the wayside. Fortunately, one or two of the good ones still pop in from time to time. I've no idea why.

'URBAN' EDDIE HAMMERMAN

Eddie first came in on the show after sending me a 50-page fax begging for work experience. As soon as he arrived, I knew he'd be trouble. The guy couldn't stop telling lies. To be fair, it was all in the name of radio entertainment but even so, it starts to bug you after a while. We nick-named him Urban Eddie due to his penchant for urban myths. He turned out to be great. At one point he tried to trick me into converting to Judaism by taking me on a night out to see what I thought was a tribute band called The Sabbath. It turned out to be a Friday night in round his place with his folks. The last straw came when he booked me in for a circumcision. Eddie is now a full time radio producer in his own right.

JON THE JESTER

Jon's an interesting case. He pretends he's Chinese and says he hails from Hong Kong. In truth it was just a ploy. We'd been banging on about never having any oriental folk write to us for work experience when this guy turned up. We haven't yet told him that we saw through his disguise on the first day. He still thinks we don't know. He's also a magician who keeps us entertained with his sleight of hand stunts. A top bloke all round.

ANDY THE BEAVER

Young Andy is the youngest work experience person ever. He was about 4 when he first came in. He's listened to nearly every show we've ever done and files them all on his computer – what an anorak. He now claims to be eighteen and still pops in during the college holidays – bless.

AMBROSE HERON

Ambrose used to fax us with film-type questions for the show. He's a bit of a buff. Eventually he winkled his way into our mighty studios and has been around ever since. He's media crazy and seems to know everything about everything. He's now our full time film critic and enjoys the trappings of premieres and celeb mixing.

Chapter 2.

Talky Bits

Over the years, the programme has experienced many evolutions. On occasions, we may just border on the serious side of life although thankfully, these moments are extremely rare. Sometimes there's a newsworthy issue that one simply can't avoid. Our main philosophy has been to indulge in subject matter that you just don't hear anywhere else. Don't get me wrong. I love serious debate and I could talk for hours on current affairs, but one has to keep in mind that there's a night time audience out there thirsty for some light relief. Whatever anyone says, people generally only remember the funny stuff. With that in mind, we've always made a conscious effort to retain a "light" approach to the programme. This in itself can bring on accusations of flippancy, schoolboy humour and even lazy broadcasting – allegations which I would refute at every level.

The most common trick for a Talk Host is to grab a couple of newspapers and read out the top three stories. Easy to do, but where's the integrity? Where's the depth or the soul? That *is* lazy broadcasting. Taking someone else's agenda and re-working it for a radio audience doesn't constitute an intelligent approach. You'd be amazed how many people think it does. Our belief is that, if you're going for the obvious newsy material, then spin the damn thing, give it another angle, turn it on its head. It's amazing that anyone can still get away with asking: "Fox hunting – what do you think?" – a question that carries zero intellectual weight and not an iota of thought. There's nothing wrong with the odd brush with the obvious and no one is saying that every single issue has to be dramatically treated before going to air, but to base an entire show on pretty much the front page of a broadsheet or a TV news bulletin is unforgivable.

What constantly amazes me are the folk who genuinely believe that by the mere action of covering a news issue, you automatically become the more seasoned and journalistically experienced broadcaster – this is cak! It takes two minutes to initiate a debate on drugs or capital punishment. It takes less than that to decide how to sell the subject. Whatever the accusations of flippancy, it can take an entire evening to put together three or four of the quirky, left-of-centre type subjects that we like to cover. These are the kinds of categories that may only get one or two callers, but they're the right callers, they're the golden nugget stories that no amount of conventional research would ever find (mainly because the subject has never come up before).

The next section is a listing of some of those 'odd' subjects that we've covered over the years. They're in no particular order but all received a top quality response and resulted in some of the funniest and most original stories I've ever heard on British Radio. If you're not familiar with the kind of show I do, you'll just have to sit and figure out what kind of tales could have possibly been promoted from the following.
For the benefit of any plagiarising radio hosts out there (and you know who you are) – nick whatever you like, we've already done 'em!

Have you ever peed next to a celebrity?
All teenage boys should visit a prostitute at least once
Does your pet talk?
Strange places you got your finger stuck
Solve the homeless problem – open up UK Kibbutzim
Did you perform surgery – on yourself?
Have you ever died and remembered it?
What does your school bully do for a living now?
Been to a night club in the North East and NOT pulled?
Pets in Pants
The National Lottery should only be for folk over sixty
Ever eaten human flesh?
Feed the homeless with a hound
All 18 yr. olds should pay 50% tax
God Vs Fireworks
The vet killed my pet
Cull the seagulls
Calati Quim – the new religion
Show us ya box
I killed a line-dancer
The great vibrator give-away
All students should be strippers
I did it in disguise
Accidents involving sparrows
Naked in the gym
Judge Dread Cops
I caught my boyfriend having a facial
Well it wasn't there last night

Cursed by the gypsy woman
The media is your new God
Well bugger me
Televised fox hunting
Dirt Bag Derby
Paramedics are too fat
Kill mice
I pretended to be in a wheelchair
I witnessed a miracle
Guess what our burglar took?
Public acts of resignation
Bring back jousting
My time as a groupie
I worked for the Queen
I got a mention in Parliament
Rhetoric Roulette
Pie or Die
They filmed it at our house
Creature of the Nightingale
Ever worn a chastity belt?
MP's in Tepees
Celebs in Beds
Esperanto is back
Guess my rellie!
Lenny Henry is my hammer
I invented that
Sheep Squeak
Flat mate voodoo

Snakey Snakey
Graffiti Rules - OK
My pet is possessed
Teach Morris Dancing in Schools
Kung Fu Freaks
Ugly animals
Famous Darrens
I made a porn movie
What is free?
Felatio Nelson
How to live on a quid
A dog ate my digit
The Canadian bear theory
Old Fart or Young and Smart
Guess what a stranger gave me?
The backstage party
What happens if I press that?
Marry ya cousin
I sabotaged a muso
Let's nick Fred's weather map
Itchy Itchy
The perfect murder
I bonked an MP
It ate my helmet
Mistaken identity
Ham & Squirrels can save the world
Bring Back Capital Letters
I lived with a Vampire

Chapter 3.

Who Calls?

There's a rather unfortunate myth that anyone who calls a radio phone-in, *must* be a fruit cake. I can only imagine this is based on the odd nutter who does call. If you're not particularly au fait with phone based formats and you happen to catch the odd programme while some muppet is in full swing, I guess it's easy to go away with that impression. It's the nut job fraternity who stand out. Sadly, you could have an entire night where your switchboard is full of quick thinkers, academics or the plain street-wise - and some folk will still only hear the bozo brigade.

Since I've worked in phone formats, I've probably spoken to some of the best of the British public and perhaps the worst too. It has to be said that the great majority of callers are there to make a valid point or contribution to a debate or idea. The range and type of people who call, fax or email is vast: Cab Drivers, Doctors, Builders, Lawyers, Lifeguards, Singers, Actors, City Boys, Painters, Plumbers, Ice-cream vendors, IT bods, Pilots, Housewives, millions of students, Political folk, Restaurateurs, Sportsmen, Nannies, Oil workers, and the list, quite literally, goes on....

I have no idea who the faces are behind the voices and no real knowledge of a caller's background or circumstances. Some people call regularly, some call only once, and others may leave a three-year gap before calling again. There's no definitive pattern. There are many ingredients to a successful phone-based programme and a bank of regular callers is, without any doubt, one of them. Although I've always been keen to avoid creating an "in-crowd" (regulars to my show can only call once a week) a staple diet of familiar callers assists both the consistency and the identity of any format. To a new listener of say a few weeks, regular contributors become as much part of the identity of a programme as those in the studio. Be they the Dink from hell or the fluent lay-philosopher, a network of verbal familiars forms a vital thread in phone-based programming. Despite the "How on earth did they get the vote" mongers out there, most regulars (be they on the phone, email or fax) are a delight to talk to and communicate with. The odd caller is a vitriolic son-of-a-gun, but I guess that's fine too. It all makes up the colourful tapestry that is UK late night radio.

I apologise to anyone who's missing from the enclosed list. Over the years, there have been so many notable contributions – thousands in fact - and inevitably it's hard to remember everyone. It's sod's law that I'll have missed out some of the most prominent. Believe me, it's nothing personal.

Roger from Bristol

All we know about Roger is that his name isn't really Roger and he wouldn't know his way around Bristol with a police escort. He's a bit of an amateur philosopher who squeaks too much. Despite his lengthy contributions he often talks crap.

Marie the American

One of our few great Yankee callers, Marie is great. A good brain and a whole bunch of life experience. She phones, faxes and emails. She also sends us lots of sweets & biscuits. She once tried to poison us with an out of date packet of bourbons.

Judith The faxer

Never calls but always faxes. She's a Geordie girl who saw sense and moved south. One of the more observant contributors. She has red hair and a penchant for men who wear plaid. Judith has many bizarre and questionable pass-times. She's currently writing a book about otter farming in Gwent.

Adrian from Liverpool

A lovely chap. He's the guy in the pub who could attack your funny muscle at a moment's notice. He's travelled, sporty and doesn't quite know what to do with his life. He recently applied for a job as a window cleaner on the West Bank.

Rainbow George

George is another great thinker. Loves alternative politics and has quirky views on everything. One of his crazy plans is to abolish money – I just hope he buys this book before he does. He's mentioned extensively in Peter Cook's biography and often crops up in the newspaper gossip columns. Sounds a bit like Dennis Norden on acid.

Cameron from Dundee

Here's a guy that brings a whole new meaning to the art of time utilisation. He's always got his nose in some book or another and wastes no time in proposing a new issue. A true Scot who has a great belief in the Euro dream. He has a tattoo on his buttocks dedicated to the show.

Rev. Alan Blizzard

The Witty Faxer. Obviously he's not really a vicar. Writer of funny scripts, and has even penned an album all about the show. We've no idea where he gets his time from, although a recent Internet rumour suggested he's actually doing a ten stretch for poultry smuggling (cock gags on a postcard to the Rev. please).

Eiblish O'Shea

One of the UK's most undiscovered talents. Despite many appearances on the Barrymore show and a weekly airing on ours, she's still yet to get a recording deal. I can't understand it, you should hear her voice. Was probably inspired by the late great Betty Swallocks.

Wilfred from County Down

"A very Good Morning to you Ian" is how Wilfred opens up his calls. Has the strongest Irish accent and despite being one of our more senior callers, a great way with women. Has a unique habit of dropping in a great phrase or line that almost kills. I'd pay to see this man chat up women, in fact *he* pays to chat up women!

Mrs Mad

Don't even ask. One minute she sounds sober, the next, slaughtered.
On occasions she's calm, most of the time she just shouts a lot. We can't work this woman out. Says she has many celebrity friends. She provides hours of amusement for the nation, sadly, at the total expense of herself.

Ann in Wolverhampton

Ann is lovely. She doesn't call as regularly as she used to but when she does, she makes up for it. Often corrects me on my grammar, sometimes she's right, although most of the time, naturally, she's wrong. She's also sent me some lovely pressies too.

Nigel in Cheltenham

An Oxbridge Graduate who's gone back for more. Has a habit of winding people up with his views on class and education. Never a dull moment. He once dated a female politician and a male model, although not, that we know of, at the same time.

Andy in Manchester

Andy first started calling after a bad car crash left him fairly sleepless. An authority on Coronation street who has an uncanny knack of bumping into cast members in the Arndale Centre. He's also close to the band "Half Man Half Biscuit". A large leap from his days as a "New Kids on the Block" fan.

Les in Eltham

Mr Conspiracy. Les has a theory on everything from why the dollar bill is designed that way to why we have fluoride in our water. He never calls, but always faxes. He could be anyone. Personally I think he's a government spy trying to infiltrate my brain. He scares me...a-lot!

Big Madge from Barnes

Madge is dynamite. The fact is, she isn't big (I've met her) but she does sound very Matron like. A lovely down to earth girl with the richest voice in town. She listens to the show naked while being pampered by Peruvian midgets.

Sumpy & Co. the Bakers

These guys are so busy baking bread for some of London's finest restaurants that they hardly get time to call these days. However, Sumpy and his crew (like us, they've changed a bit over the years) are another of the UK's great normality brigade. Sumpy has a large autographed picture of me on the side of his oven – strange.

Terry in Hitchen

A great caller even if he does talk balls. A champion, apparently, of the working classes and a passionate hater of the money gabbing filthy rich. His arguments have more holes than a gypsy's sieve. I'd love to meet him though, just to give him a bit of a slap.

Lee the Cabby

You've heard of white van man, Lee is Black Cab man. Sadly a supporter of the mighty Spurs but other than that a smashing chap. A good solid, level headed purveyor of sense. He once owned a dog who inadvertently charged at 30mph into his brand new conservatory window. Naturally, caring Lee was distraught - that glass had cost him over a grand.

Ralph the Nazi

He could be John, Ken, Bill or Kevin. This guy has come on under so many different names. A full time ultra right winger, who knows much of his history but makes the bits up he's not sure about. Usually offensive, but never dull. Probably mentally damaged somewhere along the line.

Mickey the Cabby

Another of the Cab fraternity. He's a good guy for lots of reasons but particularly for his regular trips to our studio to bring us bacon sandwiches and fizzy pop. Another Spurs fan who wears a love heart locket around his neck with a picture of Ozzie Ardilles inside – mmm.

In addition to that list, there's also...

Gator in Watford, Captain Chaos, Musical Nigel in Maidstone, The always funny Gordon in Hemel, Wattie in Edinburgh, Russ – obviously, the lovely Sue in London, Richard in Ryll, Sean, All the UK Truckers, The Golden Wonder Guys, The Royal Mail mob, The Walkers Crisps Pack, Emma in Stoke, Anita in Manchester, Dave at Doves, Bev in Edinburgh, Asif in East Ham, Del the black black cab driver, Jim in Fife – a top bloke, The always lovely Jane in Tunbridge Wells, Charlie, Sarah – yes that one, Big Mappie in Glasgow, Wendy in Norwich, Cyril, Captain Tangent, Fat Bloke, Doreen in Leeds, Sue in Weston, Muhammad, The other Charlie, Victoria in Bridgend and son, Mr Kahn, Peter in London – what at great bloke, Mario the sex guy, Alf in Bradford, Janice – you petal, The fabulous baking boys, Tony in Sussex, Manor Park Sorting Office, Judge Pickles, Geordie in Newcastle, Laurie in Bristol – the King Lives, Jenny, Bob – are you still there?, Maureen, Ruth in Dagenham – always a pleasure never a chore, Martha, Guy, Kirsty the Bold, Julie, Les, Karen – Matron, Barry the gay trucker, Lucy the delightful, Peter Chadwick from Stoke-on-Trent, the die-hard Tory, Ivan Woolhouse-Peters – where did he go? Harriet, Adrian, Gloves, Sally, Ellie – thanks for the photos, Kevin in Aberdeen, Crispy in London - the tea leaf, Margaret the delicate, the other 750 000 - oh, and YOU.

Chapter 4.

The Lists

10 OF THE MOST ANNOYING THINGS THAT CALLERS SAY

1. *'Hi, I'm a first time caller, I'm a bit nervous'* – I didn't need to know that.

2. *'You're going to cut me off aren't you?'* – for some reason there are folk out there who think the host will automatically cut their line as soon as something controversial/disagreeable is said. That's what the host wants, muppet!

3. *'You always cut people off if they get the better of you'* – that's the least likely time a host will cut the call. He usually waits until he's got the better of them!

4. *'You only put people on air that agree with you'* – nothing is more inaccurate than this one. The host craves disagreement.

5. *'Who do you think you are?'* - what kind of a Dink question is that?

6. *'Everybody hates your show'* – these remarkable people appear to have done a national survey on taste. They have a degree in talking on others' behalves.

7. *'You should be taken off the air for that remark'* – which breaks down to someone suggesting your entire livelihood should be taken away on the basis that they disagree with you. That's fair, isn't it?!

8. *'Why do you talk so much?'* – Hey, let's think about this one for a while shall we? Dink!

9. *'What gives you the right to say that?'* – how about the fact that A) I'm a citizen of this damn planet, B) It's my show!

10. *'All your callers are idiots'* - obviously apart from the bright spark making that comment. You could have a switchboard full of Oxbridge professors and some arse would still make that comment.

CREATURE FACT

When Ian interviewed Antonio Banderas, the recording equipment broke down. The problem was only solved when Antonio himself took a look and fixed it. They're clever those Latin sorts.

10 CELEBRITIES WHO'VE HOSTED SHOWS ON TALK RADIO

1. **Jeremy Beadle** – Used to do a Sunday evening programme. He'd worked in Radio long before he became a big TV face. He's one top chap.

2. **Trevor McDonald** – Hosted a short-lived current affairs weekend show. The problem when you're a National TV news reader doing a radio show is that you still have to retain your impartial stance.

3. **Steve Wright** – Didn't stay long but hosted a Saturday morning zoo show. Nice bloke all round.

4. **Terry Christian** – His weekend gig came off air within months. Can't think why.

5. **Vanessa Feltz** – In her larger days she hosted some weekend affair – I hated it and given its short run, I wasn't the only one. I met her only once. Very pink.

6. **Lorraine Kelly** – Lovely woman, used to do lunchtimes. Continues to be the face of early morning TV.

7. **Jonathan King** – Did mid-mornings for a while. I thought he was great considering he discovered "Genesis"!

8. **Lowri Turner** – Co-hosted drive time for a while before going on to a more TV based career and a baby.

9. **Nicholas Parsons** – Filled in for a few Saturday morning things. You can't stop this dude talking.

10. **Andrew Neil** – The former Sunday Times editor did some Sunday morning gigs.

CREATURE FACT

Kev the Wondersheep recently took six months out of radio to travel the world in search of spiritual nirvana. His monster trek took him from Australia to South America. He came back a changed man (and a slimmer one). During his hike he also got engaged to the lovely Karron – she must be mad.

10 CELEBRITIES WHO'VE APPEARED WITH IAN COLLINS & THE CREATURES OF THE NIGHT

1. **Hugh Grant** – top man, a total gentleman. Sadly, he didn't bring Liz.

2. **Robin Williams** – I think I only asked one question and he was away. Couldn't stop him talking. He was hilarious.

3. **Brian Cant** – The God from 70's kids TV. He was just *so* nice. Too damn nice actually and that makes me suspicious.

4. **Lois Maxwell** – Miss Moneypenny from the Bond Movies. I don't think this chick even realised we were on air!

5. **Melanie Griffiths** – One sexy woman. The interview finished early so I sat and shared a doughnut with her. Most guys would pay to see her do that.

6. **Johnny Morris** – Mr Animal Magic. Another one who appeared on our Icon's Corner feature. He was as pissed a newt throughout. Talked about monkeys a lot!

7. **Antonio Banderas** – I couldn't believe how short this guy was. He swore a lot during the interview, in a kind of Spanish type way.

8. **Alice Cooper** – I sat in a West London bar to interview Alice. The earthiest guy I've ever met. He said everyone should own the Saturday Night Fever soundtrack album!

9. **Tony Hart** – what a gentle chap. I couldn't believe I was chatting to the man who knows Morph and Chaz!

10. **Malcolm Mclaren** - Great value for money. He was a tad laid back and would perhaps have benefited from the insertion of a firework!

CREATURE FACT
Ian once double headed a radio show with a fat bloke who turned out to be a convicted criminal who had spent time in prison. The fatty concerned went on to spend more time in the slammer at a later date. What a slimeball!

10 PAST AND PRESENT CONTRIBUTORS TO THE SHOW

1. **Meg Pringle Adamson** – In my view the UK's number one numerologist and dream analyser. Meg also works as a Harley Street therapist and is the nicest person you could ever meet.

2. **Graham Whiley** – Top ghost boy. Graham is a real life ghost buster although he hates that expression. He's had more paranormal trips than Jim Morrison.

3. **Murray Grant** – Murray is a former Chippendale! He came to us as our culture guru. We sent him all over the place in search of leisure. From what we can gather, he found plenty of it.

4. **Ambrose Heron** – The best film critic in the business. This man can name virtually any detail of any film from any time. What a smart arse.

5. **Danny Wallace** – Comedy-meister extraordinaire. Dan is a leading authority on comedy. He knows virtually every stand-up in the business. He also works as a writer and is an active radio and TV producer too. One clever son-of-a-gun.

6. **Lucien Morgan** – The Archdeacon of the paranormal. Lucien was another authority on the weird. He has a voice like you never heard and the biggest hair in the world.

7. **Gary Jacobs** – One of the UK's leading lawyers and broadcasters. Gary is a 'tell it like it is' man. He's regularly appeared on the show with a series of digestible legal features.

8. **Richard Thames** – This bloke knows everything about history so we thought we'd drag him in for a regular slot. It turned out to be a highly interesting piece of broadcasting. Award winning stuff I'm sure. Riveting.

9. **Ian Royce** – Hey, it's that funny man! He's a comic, and an actor who pops in for a casual chat. Is there no beginning to this man's talents?

10. **Steve Miller** – He was our European correspondent. We used to send this guy all over the continent in search of wacky Euro news. If the budget ran out, he used to report from his bedroom and just pretend he was somewhere else.

CREATURE FACT

When Ian interviewed Robin Williams, Robin's first words were 'Hey, white man, how the F*** are ya?' Ian took about ten minutes to recover after Robin poured him a stiff mineral water.

10 CREATURE FILM RECOMMENDATIONS AS SUGGESTED BY THE TEAM & LISTENERS

1. **Natural Born Killers** - (Oliver Stone, 1994) – This should be shown in schools along with Shakespeare. Why they tried to ban this, one can only guess.

2. **Citizen Kane** - (Orson Welles, 1941) – A life changing film. Not only is it technically groundbreaking but its theme is as moving as it gets.

3. **Midnight Express** – (Alan Parker, 1980) - Drug detail a plenty. Based on a true story, this one tugs at ya morals like a rabid badger. Great ending.

4. **One Flew over the Cuckoos Nest** - (Milos Forman, 1975) – If you haven't seen this, you must have been living on mars. The human condition is wonderful!

5. **Network** - (Sidney Lumet, 1975) – The best film about TV ever. Oscar winning performances and a great insight into how the media really ticks.

6. **The Truman Show** - (Peter Weir, 1998) – Don't expect comedy Carey! This movie opens up a whole bunch of questions.

7. **Airplane** - (David Zucker, 1980) – Still one of the funniest films ever made. Watch it 10 times and you still won't catch every gag.

8. **The Parallax View** - (Alan J. Pakula, 1974) – If you're looking for something that delves into conspiracy, you won't go wrong with this one. Watch it at least twice.

9. **Rear Window** - (Alfred Hitchcock, 1954) - Classic Hitchcock stuff. Everyone talks Psycho, but this wins hands down.

10. **Jaws** - (Steven Spielberg, 1975) – Sounds almost corny now, but this really is a great movie and was years ahead of its time.

CREATURE FACT

Ian Collins was once a monster in BBC TV's Dr Who. He played a Haemovore in a couple of episodes of 'The Curse of Fenric'. During filming he had to chase a dog-collar-wearing Nicholas Parsons around a graveyard.
Sylvester McCoy was the Doctor.

10 CREATURE BOOKS RECOMMENDATIONS, AS CHOSEN BY BOTH THE TEAM AND BY LISTENERS

1. **Lolita – Vladimir Nabokov** – Everyone should read this. Another book that will tug at every moral string in your body.

2. **Strait is the Gate – André Gide** – One of the best love stories ever told. Watch out for Juliet.

3. **The Garden of Eden – Ernest Hemingway** – Pretty much his last novel. Delicate subject matter.

4. **I Bet You Won't Read This – Ian Collins** – You're holding it in your hand as we speak. Isn't it great!

5. **The Hippopotamus – Stephen Fry** – one of the funniest contemporary writers. You won't put this book down.

6. **High Fidelity – Nick Hornby** – It's every man's story. This book is hilarious and doesn't miss a detail.

7. **An Unquiet Mind – Kay Redfield Jamison** – This book is about depression but don't let that put you of. It isn't a novel, it's semi-autobiographical.

8. **The Dead – James Joyce** – Just read and enjoy.

9. **Fuzzy Monsters – Chris Horrie & Steve Clarke** – It's the inside story of the changing BBC. Compelling.

10. **Bleak House – Charles Dickens** - It'll be argued that you could pick virtually any Dickens book, but you won't go wrong with this one.

CREATURE FACT
Sarah Mulvey appears in the opening shots on the Dustin Hoffman film, "Marathon Man". She was a toddler and living in New York at the time and became a kiddy extra. Some say she looks like a young Kathleen Turner, Ian thinks she looks more like a young Ted Turner.

TEN PRESENTERS WHO'VE FILLED IN FOR IAN COLLINS AND THE CREATURES OF THE NIGHT

1. **David Banks** – Former editor of The Sunday Mirror (he's the guy that published those 'Diana in the Gym' photos) an absolutely top bloke who did a couple of fill ins over Christmas.

2. **Tara Newley** - Daughter of Joan Collins (I bet she loves people constantly mentioning that). She filled in for me one Christmas, not sure why.

3. **Chris Ashley** – One of the nicest blokes in the world. Chris has also worked on just about every radio station on the planet. A total pro. who never lets you down.

4. **Tommy Boyd** – When Tommy (who is one of the best talk hosts in the business) made his return to the National airwaves, this is where he did it – our show!

5. **Nick Abbott** – Top talk host. Nick is one of the UK's best. You either "get him" or you don't – it's cult-followed stuff. His return to the National Talk scene came when filling in for us.

6. **Mike & Miff** – Hallelujah! It took years for a programme manager to realise that if I'm away on holiday, it makes sense for Mike & Miff to present to the show.

7. **John Gaunt** – A great pair of hands to have in your seat. This guy can take a show in all directions. Exactly what you need.

8. **Mike Allen** – A seasoned pro who's been in speech radio for years. Before getting his own regular gig, he filled in for us.

9. **Ronnie Barber** – Again, one of the best. Lively, original, funny and doesn't just dwell on some boring news item in order to get a show going.

10. **Charlie Wolf** – The only yank to take the chair! I used to listen to this guy on some pirate station when I was a kid – how weird is that?

CREATURE FACT
Ian was the last radio bloke to interview the actor Peter Cushing. Peter appeared on Ian's show on more than one occasion and despite being ill at the time, never refused the invite. What a nice bloke.

10 WEIRD THINGS THAT IAN HAS BEEN SENT IN THE POST BY LISTENERS

1. **See Chapter 5** – Enough said.

2. **4 dead pheasants** – They weren't even plucked. It was a guy called Gator in Watford that sent 'em in for Christmas. We had to donate them elsewhere before they went on the turn!

3. **A used condom** – Brings a whole new meaning to things coming in the post. It must have been a guy that sent it, and doubtless he was on his own when he prepared it.

4. **A sanitary towel** – Don't even ask why some bod would want to send you that. It arrived in one of those jiffy bags with no letter. And before you ask, yes it was.

5. **Hard-core pornographic videos** – We talked about porn on air one night and the following day a huge package of filth arrived. We were naturally disturbed by this and hurriedly destroyed the lot!

6. **One pair of knickers** – There's a myth that folk in the media world receive this kind of stuff all the time. It only happened the once. The pair I received was an off-white colour and could have housed a colony of bats. Where's the romance gone?

7. **A dead spider!** - And it was quite a beast. Some nutty woman who's been writing for years (and never gives her name) decided that the love she had for me had died. The spider was her little metaphor – crazy old bag.

8. **Naked Photos** – It only happened once, honest. It was some snaps of a girl in her bath. Unfortunately there weren't enough bubbles to cover the Plimsoll line.

9. **52 stuffed toys** – These things were years old and stank. Why they were sent we don't know.

10. **A Voodoo Doll** – Fortunately it wasn't meant to be a curse on me, but someone else who will remain nameless. There are some nasty people out there kids.

CREATURE FACT
As a TV producer and director Sarah has worked on numerous projects including Talking in Class (CH.5) and Pet Rescue (CH.4).
She recently went to Paris to cover the Concorde tragedy for ITN.

Chapter 5.

Ian's Untold Story

When it comes to untold stories (as in never told on the air) I have a bit of a choice. I could tell you about the night that we thought we were going to be murdered, literally. I could re-live the tale of when one radio station fired me and re-hired me on the same day, or I could give you the full story of what happened with me and a listener in a stationery cupboard. Alternatively, there's the shameful tale of how I got out of taking part in a charity stock-car race, the real reason I cancelled a show and called in sick, or the unfortunate time when telling someone what I did for a living nearly got me arrested. As it happens, I've chosen this one.

***

As Michael Burke might say on the 999 Programme, "It was an ordinary day".

I arrived for work at about 9.30pm. I followed the usual routine: drove into the car park, jumped in the lift, said hello to the security guard and then headed for the mail room to check my post. The pigeonhole displayed a familiar sight: a bunch of internal memos, a parcel and a wad of letters from listeners. When it comes to receiving post I still get excited. Even being in a job where you might receive hundreds of letters each week, I still feel that same buzz that you get when you're about six years old, when the only time mail arrives for you personally is on your birthday. Because I read each and every letter myself, I've always found it easier to deal with correspondence before doing anything else. I grabbed a coffee and then sat at my desk to find out what delights were in that days post bag. Mike Hanson arrived and after our usual chat, I continued to read the post as Mike set to work on the show.

The letters were all fairly routine: requests for photographs, a point on the previous week's shows, enquiries about a piece of music we'd played and a few healthy suggestions for topics. The only thing left to open was the parcel. Again, the child in me returned as I sat and pondered the possibilities of its contents. It was actually more of a jiffy bag than a parcel, maybe 9 inches long and about 6 wide. The inevitable squeezing and poking of the package gave me no clues as to what might be inside. I opened it. Being fairly stereotypical in the post-opening department I performed the obligatory peek inside before finally yanking out the contents. It isn't exactly unprecedented to receive the odd bizarre present in my line of work but what I'd been sent on this day was so unusual looking I couldn't even work out what it was. For whatever reason, I instantly deposited it back into the bag, sat with it in my lap and stared at the wall. Something in my mind was computing. I could almost feel the cells of my brain searching for the correct association as if reluctantly trying to make the kind of connection they rarely need to make. It was like a prolonged double take. I pulled it out of the package again and sat it on the desk. Again, I stared at it.
'Mike, what do you think that is?' I said.
Mike was working on his computer at the time and turned around to take a look. Either Canadians have quicker brains than Brits or the boy Hanson has a covert past that I'm not privy to, because he seemed to make the same connection as me but at a rather more rapid rate of knots.

"Shit Ian, looks like a fucking bomb."
He confirmed what a tiny part of me had thought on taking that first peek inside the packet - someone had sent me a bomb.

There's no doubt that humans never stop learning. Throughout our childhood, we're taught our manners and morals, our values and our standards. In teenage years we tend to reassess those earlier indoctrinations and try to adapt them to suit our developing personalities. Sometimes we get things right, often we get things wrong, but either way we're learning all the time. In adulthood, the curves become even sharper. We learn heartache, we get to know how to deal with personal finance, we experience trauma, and we begin to formulate our ideas of a future. It's a wonderful evolution that, by definition, never stops. If you had to list, individually, everything you'd ever learnt, you couldn't do it in ten lifetimes. It's testament to that amazing device called the brain that we're able to bank, savour and recall so many experiences at will. Beautiful. However, unless I missed something in the social science class, no bastard ever taught me, or it seems Mike Hanson, how to behave when someone sends you a bomb.

This lack of ballistic knowledge was manifest in the way Hanson and I dealt with the realisation that we could, at any moment be blown through the windows of an Oxford Street radio station; we took two steps backwards.
"Do you think it's a real one?" said Mike.
" I've no idea," I replied. "I've never seen a bomb before."
I had a gut churning feeling that this grotesque device was going to explode any second. It sounds almost cheesy to say this now, but all I could think about were those closest to me, the people I loved. I wondered if they felt the same way about living without me as I did them. How on earth would they ever continue living normal lives?

The device was housed in a kind of plastic cassette-tape box. There was a battery wedged inside and the rest of the case was filled with a kind of rubbery substance (Semtex?). Protruding from the box were various wires. One moment it looked as if some no-nothing dink had made a pretty poor attempt at replicating a bomb, the next it looked like the most menacing thing in the world. Additionally, at a time when Anglo-Irish relations were still pretty tense, it didn't help that the packet had a Belfast post mark on it.

After what seemed like minutes but was probably seconds we eventually bolted up the corridor to tell security. As luck would have it, a couple of foot patrol Police Officers were on the mooch just outside our building so we called them in. We pointed them in the direction of my offending parcel.
"So what do you think it is?" I said.
"Shit," said one officer. "Looks like a fucking bomb."
You don't learn that kind of terminology on the Met. training course.
"Do you think it's real?" I enquired.
"I've no idea," he said "but we're not taking any chances. I want everyone out of this building now." He hardened the word 'now' with as much authority as he could muster.
It's at times like this you realise that programmes like 'The Bill' aren't quite as

exaggerated as one first thought. What happened next was as scary as it was impressive. The officer made one of those technical calls on his radio and within the space of about two minutes the entire building was littered with Police Officers. The girls and boys in blue set to work like ants, clearing the staff (fortunately in the evening there are only a handful of people around), checking all rooms and cupboards and making sure that we all made it onto the street in safety. For whatever reason a couple of people decided they weren't going to leave and despite being threatened with arrest were adamant that they had their jobs to do and needed to remain put. For reasons unknown the Police allowed them to stay after telling them sternly that they did so at their own risk. Why anyone with families of their own should wish to do that is beyond me. Perhaps they were just pissed that it was someone else's drama.

The sight that greeted us as we walked out onto the street was staggering. There must have been 12 fire engines, about 20 police cars and a half a dozen ambulances on standby. Both plain-clothed and uniformed police were directing pedestrians and traffic away from the surrounding buildings. The dark London night was lit with the blue lights of the emergency vehicles and the usually-noisy street was made almost unbearable by the non-stop sound of sirens. We were escorted by the police to a safe side road and told to wait. The officers didn't take their eyes off me, it was as if I was being assessed to decide whether my status was that of terrorist or target. Whatever it was I didn't like it.
Amidst the panic I could make out a couple of officers sealing off Oxford Street with police tape, and, as is usual, crowds had began to gather at the perimeter. I couldn't believe what was happening here, one of the world's most famous streets and certainly one of the Capital's busiest, was being closed all because *I* had been sent a suspect package. I felt almost stupid. Under the eye of the escorting police officers, Mike and I made some small talk and kept ourselves busy by working out what we would do on the show that night. Strange what you do in moments of emergency.

Some five minutes later a police van came hurtling around the corner with its lights and sirens in full swing. It pulled to an abrupt halt right where we were standing and a man in a suit, who looked like something from the Sweeney got out and called my name. How the hell did he know my name? The obvious explanation that my details had simply been radioed through to him by a colleague didn't register. I was taken into the back of the police van to be questioned. There was another plain clothed officer waiting inside (presumably John Thaw to the other guy's Dennis Waterman). I'm advised not to talk too much about the line of questioning that followed. All I would say is that what these officers already knew about me nearly knocked me off my perch. Their questions were totally appropriate, their conduct, professional and their nature, sympathetic. I was told that as soon as the chief bomb expert arrived he would want to ask me some more questions before he "went in". They told me he was just dealing with some Government business. Government business? Blimey! This started out as a sit-com, turned into drama and was now a feature film.

Mike and I were still waiting in the side road when the bomb expert arrived. Believe me,

when some head honcho from the bomb department makes his entrance, it isn't without its fair share of drama. Sadly, I can't tell you that he abseiled in from a helicopter because he didn't. He did however arrive in an unmarked Range Rover at about 510mph. I've no idea how fast he was going when he took the corner from Oxford Street into our side road but this Joe seemed to be out of the car before the thing had even stopped. Wearing the predictable jeans and trainers, baseball cap and designer stubble, he made his way in our direction.
"Fuck me," whispered Mike. "It's Bruce Willis."
Humour is a great leveller at times like this. I nearly wet myself.

Bomb experts, we discovered, not only love what they do, they're also acutely aware that everybody else does too. Perhaps it's the curious paradox of doing something simultaneously caring and macho that creates that interest, who knows? Either way, a fair proportion of women would rather shag a bomb disposal expert than a landscape gardener and a fair proportion of men despite deciding that those types are probably gay anyway, would secretly rather *be* a BDE than a landscape gardener.

"So who was sent the bomb?" asked Bruce.
"Me." I replied, somehow trying to do my best impression of a totally unfazed bomb recipient. (*'Hey, I get bombs everyday, nothing special about this one Bruce'*).

I explained that I didn't think it could be a real bomb because having been bounced around in the postal system it would surely have gone off by now. What a dumb arsed thing to say. Slightly amused, he informed me that terrorists do actually design their bombs and packages to do exactly that. Obvious really.

It had only been about twenty minutes since initially discovering my suspect gift. Oxford Street was still manic and the on-looking crowds had now increased. The bomb expert left us and entered the building. All we could do was wait. Only one of three things could happen here: he was either going to come out of that building telling us all it was a hoax, he was going to grab one of those groovy robot things and make the package safe, or thirdly, there'd be an enormous bang and bomb boy would end up perched on top of Eros.

The expression "It seemed like an eternity" only really comes in to play at times like this. I've no idea how long he was in there. What I do remember is that at some point an already cool looking bomb disposal expert materialised looking even cooler. Drama over, it was a fake bomb. The Police managed to get Oxford Street back to normal in a matter of minutes. Whatever the training is for these kind of procedures, it works. The professionalism of all those emergency services was an amazing thing to witness. A full forty minutes after opening my surprise package, we were back in the comfort of our building. We always knew it was fake of course, had to be. I mean, how could anyone have been taken in by that? You'd have to be soft. But hey, not us, we knew all right, oh yes, we knew.

So I've added some humour to this story. The raw fact is that it really wasn't particularly funny at the time. Joking aside, this was probably the most terrifying thing that has ever happened to me since I started working in this industry. If I were some kind of shock jock or the kind of presenter that was known for my anti-terrorist views, it might have somehow been grudgingly easier to understand. That said, I've simply no real idea why any sane person would want to send something like that to anyone.

I chose to keep this story from the airwaves for obvious reasons. Not only did I want to steer away from giving the sender the benefit of hearing their intended drama lived out on air, I also felt the timing to be wrong too. Over two years have passed since this incident and only now do I feel comfortable relaying the story - and the written word seems a far more appropriate form in which to tell this tale. When you get to the Hate Mail chapter of this book you may find it easier to categorise the kind of nut that does this sort of thing. If nothing else, you'll realise there's more than one out there.

All I would say to the person who sent it is that your little plastic package resulted in the dire misuse of some forty emergency vehicles, about a hundred police, fire fighters and ambulance crews, an inconvenience to hundreds of members of the public and, I would guess, an astronomical cost to the tax payer. More importantly, however, London, like any major city is in need of its emergency services 24 hours a day. All the key departments are stretched to almost breaking point as it is and when it comes to providing life saving help to the public, these people never stop. I hope to God that no one was in need of those services while they were attending your incident. Knowing London, they probably were.

Chapter 6.

The Gallery

This chapter is dedicated to the 'gorgeous' faces behind the voices. After looking through this lot you'll understand perfectly why they're on the radio. Over the years I've been unfortunate enough to work with some of the most odd looking folk that the human race could possibly offer. Believe me, at times, it's like working with the Adams family.

We could have filled an entire book with quirky photos of the team, but then again, who would want to sit and look at that? Instead, I've chosen a selection, giving you a rough gist of what I have to look at.

Enjoy the faces, they probably won't be seen in public again.

IAN, MIKE AND MIFF IN PUB

'WORKING' – DURING THE SHOW

SARAH AND IAN – WHY HAS SOMEONE PAINTED HIS HAIR?

KEV AND IAN PREPARING THE SHOW

'PHONE SEX'
SCOTT PRETENDING TO WORK

IAN BEATS SARAH AT TABLE FOOTBALL

IAN AFTER A SHOW - WHY IS HE LOOKING MOODY?

Chapter 7.

Poignant Moments

Dunblane Tragedy

"Gordon Bennett is recognised by some as being the First man of Tabloid journalism. He was the purveyor of the snappy headline who advocated the swift sharp style that still forms the basis for tabloid newspapers today. Despite his ideology, he once said that there are some stories that are so serious, the tabloid approach has to be put to one side".

It was these words that I used to open the show the night after 16 young children and their teacher were shot dead in a school gymnasium in Dunblane, Scotland. Whatever ideas we did have about a show that night were swiftly put on hold. When a story this tragic happens, phone-in radio becomes a kind of sounding board for the nation. We didn't book any guests, we resisted speculation and simply opened the phone lines and allowed people to talk. Everybody, it seemed, wanted to offer their condolences and have their say. I'm sure psychologists would have a field day working out why this kind of reaction happens after a national tragedy. It doesn't matter. Our show that night formed a dignified response to the worst kind of news.

Princess Diana's Death

The response to this news was unprecedented. It wasn't until the day after that we were on the air again and the reaction to the world's most photographed and talked about woman being killed, along with a friend and driver, was something none of us had expected. Mike Hanson had already said to me that rightly or wrongly, this was probably going to be the biggest news story that any of us would ever witness. I expected the story to dominate the first show; there was no way any other issue was going to creep in when a news story this big breaks. What I didn't expect were for the phone lines to be red hot for 7 solid days. This was perhaps *the* most interesting peek into the public psyche. For whatever reason, people just wanted to talk and share in what was now being described as 'National Grief'. Some, perhaps rightly, were keen to make the point that as tragic as this was, it should not be elevated above a certain status and we should all bare in mind others who lose their lives in equally devastating circumstances. The reality was that people weren't seeing it that way. Again, therapists from all corners of the psychological spectrum could theorise about what was happening here. Arguments do become circular, the same points are made time and time again, conspiracy theories are plentiful and the entire debate on Royalty reared its unfortunate head. Most comments were naturally speculative and at such an early stage it was hard for anyone to make a truly qualified point. Perhaps this is what makes it all so unfathomable. Either way and for whatever reason, a nation wanted to speak, and it did.

The 1997 General Election

The Labour landslide. I was lucky enough to be on air for the coverage of one of the most interesting and now historical election nights in recent history. I was co- presenting with my colleagues Scott Chisholm and the mighty Peter Deeley. It seemed to all that the New

Labour Party would win. Nobody, however, predicted that it would have been by quite the landslide it was. The Conservative years had, for the good or bad, shaped everyone's lives over nearly two decades. In both domestic terms and on an international level, the entire economic and political system had changed beyond recognition. Now it was time for what was being perceived as something different. I won't speculate on how or why I believe this happened, other than to say that Machiavelli probably had it right. That night saw some of the biggest names in British politics fall from grace. We saw cabinet members ousted in favour of unknown new kids, Tory strongholds slaughtered by the new 'right on' left, and a BBC news reporter become an MP in one of the dirtiest campaigns of the election. To be at the broadcasting centre of all of this was a privilege. Our studios were buzzing; MP's were being wheeled in and out, pollsters were on hand to give comment and PR experts dipped in to examine the cosmetics. We had live feeds to Westminster and reporters in the key constituencies. In addition, the phone lines remained open for comment. Mike Hanson produced this marathon event and for reasons that I've still never quite worked out, Max Clifford kept me supplied with sandwiches. I wouldn't have missed this night for anything.

Going Solo

Radio studios are precarious beasts; they sometimes breakdown. On this particular night our entire phone system decided to die. We've never been a show that is solely caller-dependent but by the same token, we've never refused point-blank to accept on-air calls either. This was a dilemma. The problem was major and our in-house engineers were unable to get to the problem until the next morning. We were naked, stripped to our broadcasting bones, and left to, well, waffle. Myself, Mike and Miff have no problem creating in-studio conversation, our entire show is based on pretty much exactly that. However, we'd never been required to talk for 3 non-stop hours without taking a call.

So what do you talk about? Well, to start with, we went for the obvious: music, films, TV and books. That filled about 20 minutes. Then there are school day memories, teenage nostalgia and your first day at work. That filled another 30 minutes (2 hours and 10 minutes to go) Um, what about home life? – yep, we talked about that too, and your first love, and your ambitions and.... to cut to the chase, we talked about every darn aspect of our collective lives. It was like three guys sat in a pub having an evening out (except half the nation was listening). The time flew by. We produced the show with relative ease although by the end we didn't feel good. Was this too self-indulgent? Did anyone care? Did we have any other option?

Over the coming days and weeks, we received hundreds of letters from listeners asking us to keep the show that way all the time. Judging by the post bag, most listeners preferred it. Naturally there was some novelty value in what happened that night and it would be difficult if not impossible to repeat the routine on a regular basis. That said, I had something confirmed to me that night that I'd always wondered about: people love the in-studio banter – it works. I guess it's like soap opera where folk can enjoy (at whatever level) the goings on of other people's lives. Perhaps there's some escapism in there too. That said, and for reasons unknown, there are some listeners who seem to believe that if you're not talking to a caller then you're somehow not doing your job. I've no idea who told them that. It's as if some bizarre mantra saying 'take-a-noth-er-call' has been etched into the very core of their minds. I've always maintained that 'talk show' doesn't necessarily equal 'phone-in show'. I couldn't begin to tell you how many debates and arguments I've had with callers who feel somehow cheated because they haven't heard a caller for ten minutes. It's almost as if it doesn't matter what the caller might have to say, as long as there's a caller on. It seems that many of those people seriously believe that our in-studio banter is all about having a private conversation that we couldn't be bothered to have off air. It's anything but that. In-studio conversations are an integral part of the format. They are there specifically to set up agendas and to assist in forming the identity of a show. Just because we're not doing the conventional phone-in sell ('*cannabis – what do you think?*'), doesn't mean that callers can't join in with a conversation. This country has so much to learn about how to be a radio audience.

The Night Nobody Listened

Radio shows are always looking for ideas, features and new angles. There are all kinds of techniques that can be used to make an agenda sound that little bit different. One such method is to add a theme to an entire show. I've always found it amazing that you can ask the question: "Where is the strangest place you've made love?" and get no response and yet if you ask the same question during a programme that has been specifically themed as "Sex Night", the phones go bananas. I conclude that at times, people just need that extra reason to call, particularly if the subject is delicate or perhaps embarrassing. Once an issue is part of a theme it seems to take on a different degree of respectability. Those looking to work in speech based radio should always remember that the way a subject is sold, is key to its success. Never look for just one way of selling an idea when you can find three or four. Nobody should ever go to air without a couple of alternative spins up their sleeve.

One day we decided we would go for the theme idea and set about planning a programme called "Quiz Night". The idea was to get people to call in on the subject of TV quiz shows: folk who'd appeared on them, the backstage secrets, folk who'd cheated on one, won a fortune, got disqualified, had their lives changed etc. etc. Essentially, we were looking for the more unusual, left of centre stories. In addition to this we had Richard Whitely from Countdown, Paul Ross, the bastion of many a quiz show and Stephen Leahey (head of Action Time TV, the biggest producers of TV quiz formats) booked in as our guests. The night was amazing. We had people who'd been disqualified from Blind Date, the backstage secrets of 15-1, a man who won a car on Bullseye and had it stolen the next day, someone who broke the wheel on The Wheel of Fortune, the list went on and on. Anyone listening in would have thought that a team of about ten researchers must have spent months trawling the nation for the best quiz show stories. It was as if every other resident in the UK had a TV tale to tell. It was pure "us"; unconventional stories on a fairly conventional theme. We'd found a winning formula here and decided to do the same thing the following week.

For the next theme we chose "Bizarre Hobbies". Our thinking was simple; if we can get quirky calls about quiz shows, what kind of gems are we going to find if we start looking for odd bods who collect Dale Winton memorabilia and folk who practise naked Morris Dancing? In order to add some meat to the show, we booked a whole bunch of guests with unconventional hobbies. We had something like fifteen people booked in to talk about their questionable pass times. As with the Quiz Night the main thread of the programme would be the unprecedented tales from listener land. The show started with a bang (we made a special opening sequence to illustrate the delights of things to come). Then I explained the premise and we cut to our first guest: a man who celebrated Christmas every day. It was highly important that we kept the guest interviews to a mere four or five minutes, after all, the real stories would come from the callers. Those phoning in would be forming the entire backbone of the show. After we'd dispensed with Mr Christmas we hit an ad-break. I dashed in to the control room to check with Mike how the calls were stacking up.

"We don't have any," he said.

"What do you mean we don't have any?" I replied.

"No one's called" he said. "Not a single damn call".

Something was desperately wrong. Maybe the switchboard was broken or the transmitters were down - whatever it was, we couldn't *not* have any calls. We quickly lined up the next guest: some fruit cake who spent his days photographing pylons. As the interview progressed I kept my eye on the switchboard – still no calls. Mike checked the technical aspect and confirmed that the lines were working fine and all the transmitters were functioning perfectly. I extended the interview with pylon boy to about 12 minutes (it must have been torture to listen to). We hit another ad-break. Still no calls. It didn't make any sense, if you can get people to call in who've shared wine with William G. Stuart and made hay with a famous quiz show host, surely we can get some bozo who collects surgical stockings to call.

It wasn't to be. I pumped the phone number more times that night than I can ever remember doing, I re-set the premise and calmly interviewed more of our guests. Nothing. This was becoming very uncomfortable and my mind was doing a thousand things. I employed the most obvious technique, I switched the angle. I was now asking if anyone happened to know of folk with weird hobbies, met someone with an odd pass time or even just read about a weirdo who whiles away the hours in recreational dubiousness - anything. Not a sausage. By half way through the show we'd exhausted two thirds of our guests. The only time a line lit up was when someone called to ask if we were actually going to bother taking any calls. We'd have loved to, but nobody called. This is when good old fashioned broadcasting paranoia starts to creep in: we must be crap, nobody is listening, the audience hate us, we want our mums!

After the programme, the autopsy. As we listened back to the tape we carefully went through every possible problem. We looked at how we'd sold the initial premise, the production of the show, my approach, the calibre of guests, we analysed everything. It seemed we'd done nothing that we wouldn't normally have done, everything about that show had fallen squarely within our normal style. There was no real answer. We came up with two possible conclusions. Our first was simple: it was just one of those nights.

Perhaps the laws of broadcasting-probability dictate that these things happen every thousand years or so. Our second thought was that maybe certain programmes are better to listen to as opposed to actively take part in, after all it wasn't as if we'd suffered the problem before.

Over the years, people still mention how much they enjoyed that particular show. For us, we lost about 6 stone between us, and nearly left the industry. The lesson? Never judge a show by how many people call in, or, never do a shitty Hobbies Night again.

The Annoyed Producer

This one is poignant because it's so unbelievable. There's nothing unusual about having a bit of a jape on our show – it happens most nights. On this particular night however, the mood was even more jovial than usual.

We used to have a security guard who worked in the building who we named Steve the Sleeve (I can't even remember why). Steve hated his job. He didn't like the hours, he found the nights long and boring and would rather have been in a pub getting slaughtered. In his own words, the only thing that kept him going was listening to us lot cracking on about this, that and the other. He was able to hear the show through the office speaker system which broadcasts the station output all day. He loved the banter between us and it wasn't uncommon to see him through the glass almost wetting himself after we'd launched into some old rant of a light hearted nature. Steve was a bit like a slim Father Christmas: white beard, big rosy cheeks and a Ho, Ho, Ho type laugh – he was also very loud. At around 4am each morning the Breakfast Show production team begins to arrive. The producer is usually the first in. On this occasion the producer was a girl who we'll call Lisa. Lisa was one of life's great arseholes. A thoroughly miserable, unsociable and unreasonable person. Her entrance each morning was nearly always the same: she'd storm in to the building, would never say good morning, she'd throw things all over the office and then, for health reasons one would presume, would sit and demolish an entire cucumber. Her routine never altered.

On this particularly morning we could see through the studio glass that Lisa was having a worse day than usual. She seemed to be talking to herself and becoming increasingly agitated. The paradox of us having an overtly humorous show that morning made the whole spectacle even funnier than usual. Unfortunately, Steve seemed to be thinking the same thing. As we peered through the window we could see the strange sight of a thoroughly mad producer on one side of the office shouting to herself and a combusting Steve the Sleeve on the other side in stitches. We were witnessing this entire fest while we were still on air. As if by magic a little speech bubble seemed to appear above Lisa's head. There was no mistaking what it said: "Right that's it, I've had enough". Like a super-charged rocket, she rose from her chair and began to make her way, busy body fashion, in the direction of our on-air studio. Shit, she was coming to see us. It's at times like this when three grown men suddenly become 13 years old again. Our minds were now ticking, what could we have possibly done to her? We'd been on air since she arrived and hadn't even ventured out of the studio. Surely she couldn't have a problem with us? She tapped in the security number on the studio door and burst in. It was like the arrival of Anthony Perkins mum in Psycho. She was apoplectic. Her face seemed to make movements that weren't particularly human, her eyes were going crazy and her mad hair looked, well, even madder. We were still on air. With all three microphones still up and with a squeal that could have shattered double glazing, she blew: "Will you lot......" Mike had the sense to quickly bring down the two microphones in the control room leaving just my mic live to continue the show. I could see that they were having heated words out there. Mike and Lisa seemed to be arguing for ages and poor Hanson was having more than a little difficulty in keeping a straight face. Eventually we hit an ad-break and I dived into the control room to get a full briefing on what the hell had just happened. The explanation was unbelievable. Lisa had requested that we be less funny on the air because by doing so we were making the security guard laugh too much which in turn was distracting her from her work. We were gobsmacked. How the hell do you accommodate that kind of request? The woman must be nuts. Aside from anything else, she'd just offered us a rather large piece of red rag.

After the break we hit the airwaves again. "This next piece of radio is for our breakfast producer Lisa", I announced. I then blew a fairly substantial raspberry into my microphone. Through the studio glass I could see the woman convulsing. Her already lizard like features seemed to transfigure into something even more grotesque. It was like the kid from the exorcist. Surely her head was going to spin any moment. On top of this Steve the Sleeve had decided that a heart attack was almost imminent as he rolled around on his chair like the laughing policeman. We all continued blowing raspberries and Lisa continued rocking around like a demented zombie. An aerial photograph of these three scenarios would have been stunning. It was like a scene from the funny farm. Lisa left the company soon afterwards. Nothing to do with us, I'm sure.

Chapter 8.

The Hate Mail

I receive on average a hundred letters a week. Most are general comments on the show and most are favourable, citing favourite moments, requesting photographs or making some healthy constructive criticism on a point made by a caller or myself.

However, from time to time the "weird mail" arrives. Although this section is entitled "Hate Mail" and forms the basis for this book, it should be said that much of it is just plain crazy. One has to read the following section with a healthy open mind. Many conclusions will be obvious i.e. some folk are just plain nuts. There are many letters to which no other conclusion can be drawn. In one sense they should be written off on that basis alone and ignored. Analysing them would be futile. They do, however, form an interesting insight in the psyche of the few - or is it the majority?

Perhaps the most worrying letters are those that come from people who "appear" to have some semblance of intelligence. The letters where the writer's lexicon includes words of more than one syllable. You sometimes have to ask yourself what prompted a person to pick up a pen, a piece of paper, write it, pop it into an envelope, slap on a stamp and trek down to a post box. It's that level of premeditation that is most worrying. Then there are the wind-up merchants. Those that simply write a snotty or abusive note in order to rile the recipient. Strangely, they don't think we know this. Either way, you have to ask yourself how much time someone has on their hands, and indeed the kind of mind they have, to even bother.

The letters selected include the most abusive, unfathomable, inaccurate, inarticulate, vitriolic and plain mad. Whatever reason someone sent them, it's an interesting peep into the psychology of a small (we hope) section of the British public. You should be aware that some of the following letters contain strong language and some content of a sexual nature. For legal reasons some letters have been edited to protect the names of innocent parties. In many cases we had no choice but to re-type letters in order to make them legible, although all original spelling mistakes and grammatical errors, words that were originally underlined or subject to a highlighting pen, have been deliberately left in. The names and addresses of those who sent them have also been removed. That said, most letters in the Hate Mail department arrive unsigned anyway, which for me dilutes a little of the writer's convictions. The other common factor in these letters is the tired and predictable phrase **"I bet you won't read this"**. Invariably, the writer will live in hope that their communication is indeed read out, presumably because they're holding out for some true Andy Warhol moment. On occasions we have read hate mail on air, most of time it's ignored or just too OTT for broadcast. In any case, for those that didn't get their bizarre words on the national airwaves, fear not! We went one better - we printed the damn things in a book!

Enjoy...

You suck and everones thinks the same as me.
Your think your so superior but your not your
crap have you got that CRAP CRAP CRAP CRAP
CRAP CRAP CRAP CRAP CRAP CRAP CRAP
CRAP CRAP CRAP CRAP CRAP CRAP CRAP
CRAP CRAP CRAP CRAP CRAP CRAP CRAP
CRAP CRAP CRAP CRAP CRAP CRAP CRAP
CRAP CRAP CRAP CRAP CRAP CRAP CRAP
CRAP CRAP CRAP CRAP CRAP CRAP CRAP
CRAP CRAP CRAP CRAP CRAP CRAP CRAP
CRAP CRAP CRAP CRAP CRAP CRAP CRAP
CRAP CRAP CRAP CRAP CRAP CRAP CRAP
CRAP CRAP CRAP CRAP CRAP CRAP CRAP
CRAP CRAP CRAP CRAP CRAP CRAP CRAP
CRAP CRAP CRAP CRAP CRAP CRAP CRAP
CRAP CRAP CRAP CRAP CRAP CRAP CRAP
CRAP CRAP CRAP CRAP CRAP CRAP CRAP
CRAP CRAP CRAP CRAP CRAP CRAP CRAP
CRAP CRAP CRAP CRAP CRAP CRAP CRAP
CRAP CRAP CRAP CRAP CRAP CRAP CRAP
CRAP CRAP CRAP CRAP CRAP CRAP CRAP
CRAP CRAP CRAP CRAP CRAP CRAP CRAP

and don't try reading this out on air because it wont
work and getting your frineds to ring and protect you
wont work eirther just fact it and fuck off

I don't listen anyomore either.

P.S will someone tell ▓▓▓▓ to look up the words Irony and Talentless in the Dictionary.

NEE ▓▓▓▓

For Ian (pants) collins.

If my pen presses through the paper it's because I'm so fucking angry at you continually disregarding my own correspondence in favour of other listeners far fucking inferior infantile letters and faxes.

You sit there in your ivory tower, on your sixty fucking grand a year, spouting your oh so non political viewpoint as if we're all hanging on your every fucking mid atlantic affected accented work. Well I know that every listener hates you and even the people you call friends think you're a twat and never flush when they do a dump in your toilet.

Sarah, you sad misguided bint with your pseudo suppressed lesbo tendencies and that, aren't I so fucking erudite and middle to upper class superior manner. There you are prattling some dungaree and turkey baster feminist claptrap as if it all has a deep philosophical meaning. Well muzz, let me tell you, shave off the moustache, touch your toes and wink for the camera.

Pete, the telephonist cum fucking producer, you couldn't produce spittle you tight white T-shirted bandit. Your ineptitude at living the bourgois punk student lifestyle casts you, to the people who know you, as the fucking nerd who's best not heard. Why don't you try a job that will suit your intellect, you fucking chicken nugget dispenser

see ya! ʊ̈

I HOPE YOU LOSE YOUR LIFE.
YOU HAVE NO RIGHT TO LIVE.
YOU'RE GOING TO DIE.
IT WONT BE VERY NICE.

is that you have the cheek to call yourself the voice of the common man. Voice of the common prick more like. You should go back to teaching people how to drive car

radio today. Can I also make a complaint about Ian Collins. I don't think he should be presenting his show. He isn't even married, so wheres his experience? Could you also

Psycho-loser & the creatures of the shite

   Collins, for all your so called coveted education, psycho-logy, being the easiest to achieve, your cloth ears & woolly brain cells could not decipher the difference between an accordion & a harmonica. If you can get that blatantly wrong, what other gaffes Mr all Seeing Eye perfectionist? You crass so called academics are on some massive superiority trip, whereby, just because you've aped, mimicked & regurgitated prescribed indoctrination, you think it somehow qualifies you to dictate the terms to others, who did not elect an academic route; obscurum per obsurius in cloaca. As for you lot getting married, perish the thought. You, psycho-loser would want an intelligent woman. No woman would tolerate you. Is it any wonder you remain unmarried? You have no generosity in you and no love.

As for that brainless brawn and waste of time Daniels, not exactly brain of Britain or one of the bright sparks in the cosmos. Hardly an intellectual philosopher, where was he when the brain cells were being handed out? How dare that low-life be derisory about Aussie music when his previous efforts have been an assault on the senses. Having miff or muff as your sidekick says everything.

My sympathies are for the poor misguided & deluded bastards entangled and enmeshed in your tainted & poisonous ideology; straight A's for arsewipes in impotence, ripping off clothes and conveying of semen, before penetration. All climax. Complete heads up your own orifice jerks. Psycho, your no expert on aboriginal artwork. What gives you such

              Cont.

bigoted rights to judge something you know nothing about with your wankers degree in psychology and your fartist mentality. As for bomber Harris, he's so gullible & empty-headed with his nappy head effluence of bilge. A vomiting projectile of your chapter and verse. You deserve the faut de mieux of your incestuous clique, for the genuine article of a real McCoy relationship, (psycho will retain the brown trousers) with real people, is too elusive & too rich for your vile and contaminated and polluted infested systems and worm eaten mentalities. Swiss cheese for brains.

The acrid foul stench of burning rubber, nauseatingly surrounds the pathetic supercherie Sarah, like a leaden nimbus, whilst she attempts to compete with you dickheads. Give a chimpanzee a typewriter and it will eventually produce the complete works of Shakespeare or Bacon. The difference between intelligence and education is a little too subtle for you insensitive, insidious, reprobate scumbags to appreciate, and obviously wasted on you, swimming in the lower end of the gene pool. Hasta lavista suckers.

You media morons are so inflammatory, whipping up your racial hatred against non-whites. It's all right for those whites coming to the UK and sucking on the system & never making a contribution. But being in the pay, the club, the elite, you are not allowed to be critical & independent, your job is to promote government propaganda, like it's your own ideas.
If your Christianity crap was real we would all be brothers and sisters in unity as one through your idol.

Hello Horny Boy!

I promised I'd write didn't I? I never let people down. I certainly wouldn't let you down sweet thing. Ever since I saw you at that shopping centre, I knew I wouldn't let you down. So when are we going to meet? I know you like people being open and honest. Believe me, I'd be open for you any day. If you like I could come to the radio studio while you're on air. I want to give you the best sex you've ever had.

Imagine as you're talking to your callers, I could be in the corner just getting ready for the action to come. You'd see me with my legs apart and my little knickers pulled to one side just gently playing with myself as you get hotter and hotter.

I'll be so wet and you'll be so hot. You won't be able to take it anymore, and you nearly explode as I make my way under the desk with my lips formed in a perfect O. No one will know but us, and as I take your full length in to my mouth, you wont know what to do, because you're still working. But I'm playing.

Then you can put some music on or something as our lips meet and we kiss passionately. By now I'm almost naked, apart from my underwear which you soon remove. You then bend me over your desk and take me from behind like I've never felt before. I can feel every part of you inside me as our 2 bodies explode. We don't want to stop. I can grab your balls from between my legs and you come again.
So what do you say?
I'm ready when you are. Just call me!

xxxx

If you think you're so brave then why not meet me outside? You wouldn't you arsehole. Not ~~~~ unless you had your stupid mates with you, and even then you wouldn't.

It's a good job you don't go on who wants to be a millionaire you wouldn't be able to phone a friend - you don't have any HA HA

WHY DON'T YOU FUCK OFF BACK TO TESCO'S AND LET CHRIS EVANS TAKE OVER. YOU USELESS SACK OF SHIT......

Ian Collins

On your show around the 23rd on the issue of asylum seekers, you said no matter how poor these people are in their own country they only come here in desperation and they hate tearing themselves away from their homeland and friends and family.
Sorry Ian but let me tell you what these opportunist conmen are doing at this moronic countries expense. Once they are in and find a job of some sort, they only need to work here for 2 months in what is luxury compared to their land and they have sufficient money to fly £89 one way back to Zagreb or wherever and live like like kings for 9 months. What heartbreak that must be, this is what asylum means, handouts, a job and then carte blanche to do whatever they fucking well like.

If someone offered me the chance to go to Monte Carlo free board and lodgings £1000 a week when I got work and then a flight back home whenever I got sick of it, I would shout ASYLUM!

What do you think of that Collins - you brainless knob

to talk. So spastic brain-man give us a bit more of your lovely wisdom. Please remember what I said. Just you mention ▬▬▬▬▬ once more, I'll make sure I'm there before you know it. I don't care if it has to take three us to hold you down and kick the shit out of you just so long as we shut your pathetic mouth up for long enough. You haven't even got a clue

You will go to hell and so will all your friends. They should replace you with Alex Lester from radio 2 he show you a thing or two.

I hope your bollocks fall off right in the middle of your first shag. That might wipe the smile of your face. If

Dear Mr Collins

Please allow me to make some comment on you and your programme without you resorting to the privilege of the air waves to respond in a juvenile manner. Having said that, I doubt that you would read this on air anyway. I don't think your ego would stomach it.

I live alone and listen to your station most days and especially at night. I enjoy almost everything. Sometimes the odd comment is made that I don't agree with but that's all part of the reason I listen. Given that I'm open minded enough to enjoy all the other programmes, why is it that I shudder when you come on the radio? I know you're going to be very hurt by me saying this but your standard of broadcasting is simply not up to the pace of those who you work with. I've no idea why you wish to create a pub culture in a radio station. I'm big enough and wise enough and perhaps ugly enough to take most things on the chin and even laugh with the rest of them at something funny or even teasy, but I've never heard anything like the kind of rubbish, that you call radio, churned out by you.

I fear that your time won't be very long Ian. Nobody can continue spouting the type of nonsense that you do every night on the radio and get away with it for very long. You say you have the biggest listening audience, well all I can say is what a sad day for the British public if they all listen to you. Some can get away with being risky but I'm afraid you can't. Everytime you open your mouth I cringe at what you're about to say. The other day you were laughing about a cat that got stuck in a spin dryer. Why on earth do you think that is funny? If you can't have any respect for other people I would have thought that even you could have some for animals that have done nothing to you.

I also fear that you're not a particularly popular person with your colleagues – am I right there? I get the impression that you're not popular with many people. Do you have any friends Ian? I would doubt it with the way you behave. I don't imagine you had much of a home life growing up and I suppose this is your revenge. You take the Mickey out of people just to get your own back for your bad upbringing. One of your colleagues once said that you left school when you were 12 years old and went to work in a slaughterhouse. I can quite believe this. I can see you chopping up meat all-day and enjoying it.

Leaving school at such an early age is evident in the way you speak to people and your lack of compassion for others. I've never once heard you be nice to a caller and I've never once heard your show and not had to endure you putting the phone down on people when they get mad. Why don't you take that many calls anyway? Are you afraid that they'll get the better of the young butcher boy? We can't have that can we.

Before I retired I worked with some people like you. Some are beyond help. I fear you are too. I fear you're damaged and that makes you dangerous for the radio. Do you know people on the radio sound better if they smile when they speak. I heard Ian Harkness say that once. I've never even heard you laugh. There's no sense of humour there at all and at night you need one. Do you not have a sense of humour at all Ian? I sent a letter to your boss telling him to sack you because you upset too many of the older people. I didn't hear anything back. Maybe the boss is your dad. Although I would be surprised if you even talk to your family. If you left home at that age there must have been a reason. No one your age leaves home at 12.

I expect you'll throw this letter in the bin. That's up to you. I've spoken on behalf of many people in this letter. People who I know would agree with me if I asked them. I won't be listening to you or your station any more. I can find more to do at my age than you could at yours.
I'm sure about that.

My name is Tarka — not the otter, the other one.

I hope you are well on this day of fineness. I greet you with my special code. There, I bet you enjoyed that.

How many today Ian? Just say and they'll be there.

Ever tried plucking lions — they don't like it. Sometimes they roar loudly. My friend was eaten by one once and I had to put my hand down its throat to get him back, I couldn't reach so I put my other hand up his arse. I kind of stood there for a while with this lion on each arm. I could shake my own hands. It was like I was wearing one of those winter muff things. The lion looked bleak at this intrusion of his orifices. Wouldn't you?

Yesterday I went walking with a ladybird, not one of the singers, the little buzzy thing. How come it walks slower if it has more legs? You might say it's because its legs are only short. Ah, but I have no legs, just this one table leg glued to my under carriage — I kind of hop. I thought lady birds could fly. This one didn't, not after I hoped on the thing with my wooden stub. I didn't mean to.

Is Anna Ford related to any of the following — Gerald Ford, Glenn Ford, Betty ford, Gloria Estafan? You spotted the mistake there didn't you? That's right, Gerald Ford was only his married name.

If beans mean Heinz what does carrots mean?

When I was a kid my parents bought me hard lumps of rubber for Christmas and told me it was a new craze called Play Don't. The time ticketh, I must go yonder now — into the mist. Good bye lovely Creatures, 'till the next time.

Split don't spit.

Tarka

Ian Collins and the creatures of the night
They sit on the radio and talk bollocks and shite
They think they're so special in their radio chairs
What they don't realise, is that nobody cares

They talk about politics, they talk about cars
They talk old men in raincoats and women in bras
Their chat is inane, it's quite plain to see
Who calls these daft fuckers, certainly not me

One is a cockney, one is a yank
The other from Kent where the best of em wank
This trio of arse holes is as bad as can be
They don't entertain you, they don't entertain me

So why do we listen to this pile of toss
There's a radio choice, we could just turn em off
It's probably disbelief that keeps us awake
At this crappy old show of a radio mistake

Love the show really. Hope you like it boys, I told you
I wasn't much of a poet. I'll have a better one next week

hanG tHe DJ

Collins my man, you're a nice bloke, I can tell that. My missus reckons you're a bit of all right. So if ya do ever go swinging then come with us. If I have to watch a bloke shag the wife, then I'd rather it was you. I've seen her with other girls but not yet dared to see her do the full - monty with a geezer. So if you ever go for it, give me a phone. I couldn't watch her with half my dirty bastard mate

DEAR MR COLLINS

It has rose to my attention that you and your collective colleagues Miff, Sarah etc etc have now got to finally stand down now that the year 2000 has finally dawned upon us, I know this letter will upset you and will not be read out on air. But I felt I had to put pen to paper for your own good.

I think you'll find that your small amount of listeners will agree with me if this letter was to be read out, but please Ian, stop and think and consult your colleagues on the words that have sadly arisen. Sorry

    Yours thoughtfully

                    <u>Good Luck</u>

We are tired of you Jewboys and Jewgirls slagging off the older people.

Your father must be up sixty and your mother is a long way from twenty one.

One day you MIGHT? Be old and then you will know what its like to be abused regarding age.

Remember, you come from the womb. You can't get away with saying that men and woman are different species because we're not. The woman makes the man, he feeds from her and without that, there's no man. She is ALL powerful not him, so get used to it. You would be nothing without your mother,

You Jews have got <u>Too</u> Powerful Here

Ian Collins

Someone has to tell you just how bad you are. I've never heard a more egotistical person on British Radio in my life. One day I might be able to turn on your programme and not hear you cut people off just to get the better of them.

What is it that you are scared of? I might as well tell you now you have no talent so it can't be that. You also have no sense of humour and lack any sort of intelligence. I would shudder to think what your home life is like. I can't imagine your family would even talk to you. Who would want you as a son any way? I would disown you if you were related to me. I bet you've never had a girlfriend and probably never will – you're a sad pathetic excuse for a human. Someone just has to tell you. I think keeping your hands away from your own pants might be a start – there are too many of those in this world – we don't need another.

I can't see your bosses giving you another contract – which will please the nation. It's about time you had a taste of what hardship is – Mr £100 000 a year sad man.

I hope you lose your house as well as any dignity you think you have. You deserve the gutter – bad luck all round I think – lose everything and then you can experience a little of what being human is. Good luck and enjoy your holiday.

Collins

How much longer has the nation got to put up with the crap you speak? Nobody fucking listens mate - haven't you got that yet? That's why nobody calls you and that's why your going to get the sack and your contract won't be renewed.

I bumped into one of your other djs the other day ▬▬ ▬▬ and he thinks your full of shit too. Oh well bye bye Ian I'm sure you'll get a job on clit fm or some other fanny's radio station. You're just like your showbiz pal ▬▬ ▬▬ he talks bollocks to. Do you think that people want to hear about your mum or dad, who fucking cares? Nobody cares because nobody listens.

Who is your mate big rach that your always going on about?? are you in her knickers? I doubt it - NO ONE would let you in their knickers. Your probably carry aids after being up the arse of your mates you've got in there with you. I WAS SACKED ONCE AND IT AINT A NICE FEELING. Your about to feel that. I hope you loose everything. At least we won't have to put up with you and your pratt callers anymore.

▬▬▬▬
   ▬▬▬▬

> POSTAGE
> 2 HQ
>
> ROSES ARE RED
> VIOLETS ARE BLUE
> WE DON'T LISTEN ANYMORE
> SO FUCK YOU!

> Hey Ian – any chance of a shag?
> I'm tall, blonde, curvaceous and
> stunning. We could do 'things
> together. By the way, my name
> Jim and I'm packing a good ten
> Inches. Thought I should mention
> That bit. Call me big fella????????
> We also left my number at your

DEAR IAN,

I SOMETIMES ENJOY YOUR PROGRAMME. YOU CERTAINLY HAVE A FLAIR FOR BROADCASTING.

I HAVE TO SAY THAT I THINK YOUR RADIO STATION HAS LOST ITS WAY AND SHOULD MAKE IMPROVEMENTS BEFORE IT'S TOO LATE. THEY COULD START BY REPLACING YOU WITH MIKE ALLEN. I LIKE YOU IAN AND I THINK ONE DAY YOU'LL BE READY TO GO ON NATIONAL RADIO WITH A REALLY GOOD SHOW.

I THINK LIFE EXPERIENCE IS PERHAPS THE BIGGEST QUALIFICATION FOR YOUR JOB AND SADLY THAT'S SOMETHING YOU DON'T YET HAVE. YOU ARE, IF ANYTHING, TOO YOUNG FOR THE JOB (THERE IS A COMPLIMENT IN THERE) MIKE IS FAR OLDER AND THEREFORE HAS A STORY TOO TELL. I THINK IF YOU ASK, YOU'LL FIND THAT LISTENERS WANT EXPERIENCE NOT YOUTH. I HOPE YOU DON'T MIND ME POINTING THIS OUT.

IT WOULD HONOURABLE OF YOU IF YOU LEFT AND MADE WAY FOR SOMEONE ELSE.

YOURS FAITHFULLY,

Hello Mr C,

Great show, I'm now addicted. One question - why do you surround yourself with so many idiots? I'm a 25 year old Oxbridge (I'm not telling which) graduate and from listening to you, my guess would be that you also studied at one of the three 'big ones' (Edinburgh being the other in case you're wondering).

I've only been listening for a few weeks so perhaps I'm missing something. I love your style and your wit (your way of dealing with that rather odd man the other day was fabulous, can't remember names) you have a great knowledge of literature and philosophy - which is my little forte, and your programme seems to have that wonderful habit of appearing to be in the room with you – chose your own philosophical leaning on that one! However, I don't understand why someone like you would wish to surround yourself with a cockney who sounds as if he's had his brain removed and Perry the teenager who wouldn't know life if it jumped up and bit him. I'm not a snob, but I get the distinct impression that your programme should be aimed at the more intelligent sector of the British public. I fail to see how you can fully achieve that if you work alongside that inept pairing.

Please keep up the great show – I'm up working on a project at the moment which has decided to take over my life – but please do your own thing and lose the monkeys.

From

Dear C▬

Are you paid by the wankiest calls?
If you are you'd be rich. It's one thing
having a twat hosting the show, let alone
a bunch of twats calling in.

All we've had lately are discussions and
phone ins about shite. Europe, sex, pub culture
and fucking books. Are you paid by whsmiths
or something? Get a fucking life Collins.

Are you shagging that girl in your studio?
You should shag her to death. She's another
mouthy no nothing bitch.

Have a nice life wanker. ▬

There's not even any point!!

I shall probably regret writing this letter – but at the moment all I need in my life apart from death is to tell you a few things – things I'm almost 1000% sure you know and, now I've got this low ebb – it matters not what you think of me – I DON'T FUCKING CARE!!

In the beginning it was exciting – it was fun – it was a secret. I didn't even think about our age gap – I was so much in love with you – I couldn't add such a thing as 36 years in to such a special equation & later when you reminded me of all the faults we have and giggled and worst of all let that PIECE OF SLIME ▓▓▓▓ ▓▓▓▓ poke fun at me, I decided to continue to win your affections.

After I moved and my on going tragic circumstances continued, when I did tune in from time to time you sounded as if you had been stalked and violated and deprived of your dignity and you expressed this to many of your friends – whole fucking masses of them. I'm not going to talk about the loss of my friends, they matter no more to me. All humans are of little consequence, I trust no one.

If this sounds to you like some old granny having a crush on a radio person – W-E-L-L who knows. I'm in the right place. Maybe I should be in the funny farm, should our conversations ever develop that way. Before I get too old and senile to inform you what a gutless swine you are, I don't mind if you get your lawyer friends ▓▓▓▓ ▓▓▓▓ ▓▓ ▓▓▓▓▓ against me.
Do your fucking arsehole worst!
You, above all people in my life are the worst I've 'slipped' on

Hi,

It's me ▬▬ from the other night, how could you forget.

I'm glad you took my call the other night. The question is, will you follow it up?

I hope you're not all mouth and no trousers! If you want to call me you can — anytime. Why don't you ring me after the show and we can talk in all the real detail that we can't talk about on the air. I felt so bloody good after that call, I can only dream of more and better things. If you want to see me, as I said, you can come around anytime you like - after your show could be really fun, then I've got all night to feel frustrated until you get here. Now that is horny. I'm not some mad saddo, I hope you noticed that from my call, but I do think you're an incredibly sexy guy with a great voice and the looks to match. I don't want to hold you to anything but if you want me to be honest, I'd just love to f▬▬ you – badly!

Here's my number, please call. ▬▬▬▬▬
Sweet dreams sexy boy

▬▬▬ x x x x

Ian,

Every time the subject of you being homophobic comes up, you go mad and defend your corner (protest too much etc.). Homophobia is as bad as any other 'ism' (an expression you would use) and that's the point you fail to grasp. What to you is fun and harmless schoolboy humour is to many deeply offensive. Jokes about 'Chocolate Star fish' or 'Pink sheriff's badge' are just the same as minority jokes that were made on Love Thy Neighbour in the 1970's and you wouldn't say they were funny — in fact I've heard you talk about how gobsmacked you are at that kind of humour.

Being gay is a matter of basic sexuality, no more mysterious than your own. Why does that entitle you to make fun? You may not know this but you are in fact a homophobe of the worst kind. Those that are blatant are far easier to cope with because we know where and who they are. You are subtler, and that's what scares me. I appreciate that as someone, who was brought up on a council estate, you're not exactly going to be the greatest brain in the world (do you ever read a book, or do you just watch soap operas and quiz shows) but I would have thought that even a know nothing idiot like you could grasp the idea of basic offence. It's just unnecessary.

If you admit you're anti-gay you can start to deal with it, but until you do you'll simply continue with your fixed middle-class ideas. Forget your big pay packet and your adoring female fans and spare just a small thought for an innocent and much maligned section of your fellow human race.
I will come on air and say all of this if you want.

Yours,

So the gay loving Mr Collins strikes again. Welcome to Arse bandit radio.
One day we might be able to turn on your show and not hear you doing ANOTHER phone in on Homo's. You even call yourself hero of the Homo, like your some gay-fucking icon like Shirley Bassey. I don't think so. You're a wanna be fag. I believe that's what your colleague ■■■ ■■■■■ would call an apprentice turd burglar!!

If it's so acceptable to root a mans rear canal them why don't you just go on air and say you've had more of it than Quintin Crisp. Your fag audience would love that. Then you might be the hero of the homos.
While I'm on the subject, is there any chance you could get an earlier shift. It's just that I work nights and could really do without your bollocks being spewed out of the radio. I notice you have a lesbian working with you to. Is she part of your UP THE AVENUE BRIGADE?

When you first came on I bet my mates you wouldn't last the month. That was years ago and your still wanking on the air to this day. Is your boss part of the dirty crack brigade as well???
I don't think you'll answer my letter, but them again who wants to receive a contaminated letter from the king of the cock-s■■■■■

Fucked off in Hatfield

Can you tell whoever answers the phone to go and swivel on some ones fingers? What the fuck are you lot running there, a Chinese laundry. Your like the cast of Coronation street with all the bollocks you lot talk. There are actually some of us out there with a brain who have a decent point to make — do you actually realise that. I've tried so many times to make a really quick point and every time I call I get the sa[me]

Ian. I'm a lesbian and you're not, isn't that the real problem here Mr C ?

Looking at the photo of you
I've enclosed a leaflet about balding men
I think you might find it useful!

Dear Ian

I am sorry but someone has to tell you this, You are an out an out bigoted racist albeit in denial. Why else would you hold a phone in that was way out of your political depth, if not to reinforce your inate predijudices. After stirring up anger and bitterness of a black guy (who incidentally you could not match) you go on to bad mouth him calling <u>him</u> bigoted and paranoid after he'd put the phone down.
This is a little ploy of yours which shows you up for what you are. Mocking callers or slagging them off to the next idiot that gets on air (surprise-surprise) who agrees with you. And you tell us that calls are not stacked! Incidentally how many black people work on your show. Why would you surround yourself with a skinhead 'geezer' who genuflects to you and doesn't have an original idea in his head. He just will not put anyone through who he thinks will hold you in an argument – you've got him well trained.
I understand you originated from Kent – I rest my case – the home of red neck oiks, in-bred phillistines who know the price of everything and the value of nowt! The NF's spiritual home!!!
Anyone who watches TFI Friday can tell that you have lifted Chris Evans programme lock stock and Barrel but Miff is no Jamie and Sarah trying to do a Holly hotlips – forget it. Where's your original ideas.
Does Miff have a problem with his sexuality? He certainly lived up to his name and was MIFFED the other day when a caller quoted the OED, which stated that the word cockney was a derivation of the word Flower Girl.
We are a group of 12 living together in a hostel. I think we might know life a little better than you lot. Saw you Ian on Watchdog on TV the other day, like the Lord of the Manner in your posh riverside half a million pound penthouse. Do you think most of your listeners have that? We don't. Are you shacked up in there with a nice girl Ian – I don't think so.
I notice you don't get women proposition you on air like the others. People recognise real masculinity. Not you lot.
From

Dear Ian Collins

I don't suppose for one moment that you will read this out on air. I'd like to enquire as to your qualifications for presenting the show you do. The other evening you were discussing single parents. I gather you are not one, which begs the question as to why you should raise the subject. The other day a similar thing happened.

You were talking about Gulf War Syndrome. I appreciate that you were not in the gulf but have you ever been in the armed forces? I doubt it. My husband served for 25 years and could teach you a thing or two.

I know you won't read this out on air, although if you do you will no doubt ridicule me. I can assure you I'm no fool and am qualified in more areas of life than most. You should think before you start debates.

Thank you

████ ████ (Mrs)

All your callers are c___ – they can't even string a decent sentence together without fucking up every time. Is it because we have the knob of Britain hosting the show. Maybe it takes one to know one. I've heard some pricks in my time, but listening to the wanky nonsense that you lot pump out really takes the biscuit. You do have an option Mr voice of the common man – you could always do us all a huge favour and get the fuck out of that chair and let someone who hasn't got a rats turd for a brain take over.

Loved it the other day when you didn't even know that spaghetti was from Italy. I knew that when I was coming out of my dad's knob and that was 30 years ago. Did you know that the Eiffel tower is in Paris. Probably not, you probably thought it was in east London where you live like the fucking gypo's dog that you are. I'm going to tape the next show you do and then play it back to my kids so they can here what a real twat sounds like. Maybe that'll be the most useful thing you ever did, teaching kids not to grow up like you – fuckwit.

Dear Ian Collins

If brains were taxed, you be on a huge rebate by now. I can't recall the last time I heard such inane nonsense on the radio. It's more than clear that you're not particularly intelligent, but perhaps what's clearer is that you have not a shred of patriotism or feel for your national identity.

When I first heard your show, you were arguing with a black woman about racism. It seemed painfully obvious to me that 'she' was the racist - a point you didn't even mention. When the next caller came on and rightly called her a silly old cow, you cut him off and told him to call back when he'd managed to remove his penis from his forehead. I'm sure this made your friends laugh but the point is more serious. He was a British caller, sticking up for British rights, you just didn't give him a chance. So is this what happens, black callers good, white callers bad? Is that the new format? I did think I would give you the benefit of the doubt and listen again, but the next time I tuned in, the same kind of thing was happening. You had an Iranian girl call in and you flirted with her to the point that I nearly vomited (have you ever read anything on the genetic horrors of mixed race relationships - obviously not!) Can you tell me, is this British radio or Foreigners radio?

I don't mind people from all walks of life, but let's keep this country British. I think You'll find you'll get better calls if people thought you believed in your own land. Asylum seekers are part of a big business by the way, not oppressed individuals.

Come on Ian, get a life. I bet you'll never read this out on air.

PS

Dear Jan

Are you sponsored by the Scottish tourist board? I've scarcely heard a programme that blatantly sets out to fill the switchboard with so many Scots.

You tirelessly talk about what a fantastic country Scotland is and how their culture is more identified than that of the English or Welsh. Having listened to your programme, I gather you yourself are not Scottish. I wonder if you have some of it in your blood somewhere. All I know is that night after night, half your calls are from Edinburgh, Glasgow or some other town north of the border. Given the small amount of people that live there in comparison to the overall UK population I find it staggering that you have so many on air. They all seem to love you and what you do and you seem to enjoy their calls.

Given all the above factors, have you ever considered packing your bags and going to live there. I think you and the Jocks would make a perfect match. You seem to have their thinking. I also think ██████████
████████████████████████

I doubt this letter will ever reach the airwaves. If it did, you'd be bombarded by people like myself agreeing with me and not your favoured kilted morons.

The Friends of St George

▬▬▬▬▬▬▬▬▬▬▬▬▬ ▬▬▬▬▬

Derbyshire

To Ian Collins

Do you have any understanding of your fellow human beings? Who on earth do you think you are? Your programme is crass, insensitive and obscene. I have written to the Radio Authority in the hope of getting you removed. You're always going on about what makes the world tick and why we are here and which philosopher said what to whom.

If you bothered to pick up a bible from time to time, every answer you ever wanted is there. Of course you won't do this because it won't suit you to do so. If you had all the answers, you'd have no show. Isn't this perhaps what you're really scared of?

The other day a lovely woman called you to sing a song. All you did (and I can hardly believe this) was make silly rude wind noises and animal noises in the background while she was doing her best to sing for you. Do you really think that was very nice? I certainly don't and neither do my friends. Show some humility and understanding and find your God. Your programme is the lowest thing I've ever heard. What makes you think you should be allowed to get away with it and get paid for it. I hope your bosses see some good sense and take you off the radio. You can't be trusted and I for one won't be listening anymore.

Please take notice of this and grow up.

▬▬▬ ▬▬▬▬

Dear Ian,

The chancing of you reading this out on air are slim.

Is it because you've got a famous dad that sometimes appear to just ignoring all my letters?
People can be more than a little funny with conspiracy theories and so maybe you're just trying to stay out of the troubles.

Anyway Ian, I'd like to put foreword my theory about Mr. John Major. Possibly you have the same ideas as I have but don't want to say them. I understand if you don't. If JM had got into power by the true process of democracy then I don't think he would be there.

My research tells me that he is also a member of the Natural- Law party. They are the people behind him and nobody knows this (or will say) I think Norma is one too. If you don't speak out then how can I ever let people know that we've all been duped by the system. This is the way they work. They make you think one thing but are secretly doing something else.

I do understand about your dad but please let people know for the sake of our country. Our kids WILL be taught the mantra of the NL party In schools and no one sees it apart from me please read my document and write back soon with your views.

To Ian Collins the Dick of the night

I wish you were disabled, then you would know what life is really like. It must be great sitting in your fucking ivory tower talking shit all night. Do you ever stop to think of those people who haven't got a job or a life? The other day you did a phone in on people who are on a downer didn't that wake you up? Moron!

You need a great big bloke to hit you round the head with a mallet and permanently brain damage you, that might get you thinking a bit abot the rest of us.

I'm sending this letter to Sara as well she might just kick some sense into your

Thick skull.

███████ with more brains than you twats

**IAN AND THE CREATURES
SUCK
LIKE A FUCKING DYSON
HAPPY DAYS ARE
HERE AGAIN
JEW LOVER**

all roads lead to hell.
Hell is a place where
you live, a place where
you all fuck each other
in the arse and a place
where your seaman is
contaminated from the
drains of the sewers of
this great country. Have
a nice life. Once you ha

When I called to go on air, they said the lines were busy and you couldn't fit me in. Then when I called back they said you'd moved on from that subject. I called back again and was told that because some poxy guest you had on I still couldn't go on the show. What is this the friends of Collins show? What are you scared of exactly?

And why do you never put any one on that disagrees with you. Every night you have all your friends on and it's the same people every single night and all they do is agree with you and lick your arse. I thought this was supposed to be radio for the people not radio for your family. Is this just a way of getting money out of the phone calls? I wonder. Are you on a commission for every one that phones you?

And then you don't let them on you just the money. When your programme started you were OK, now your just up your own arse and crap. You never let people get a word in edgeways and you patronise the people when they call you up. I bet your family would be proud to know that they managed to breed a moron with no brian and no idea. My radio wont be on again so there's one more you've lost.

To all ~~Three Dorks~~ (that's your new word)
You really are showing how upset you all are and it's ~~pathetic~~. For the First time since your station started I turned to ~~another station~~. Ian you started all this ~~before~~ you even came to this station. The same happened with ████, why? You ~~must~~ except that other presenters are ~~top~~, you can ~~only dream~~ of being top, it will ~~never~~ happen.
You will always be ~~Little Mr Average~~ in your ~~work~~ and ~~private life~~!!!!!!!!!!!!!
A caller mentioned you never had any guests on your show, you never did answer the question as to why. I will now tell you why. Because Ian ~~Your Brain Is Not Big Enough~~ to handle any in depth topics you showed that when you tried to fill the day spots, you just haven't got it, so next time instead of slagging ████ of to the callers Tell them you just can't handle any guest's.
What it is Ian is that your colleagues have all you want and your time is running out. ~~They have nice wives~~ and you don't even have a girlfriend (+never will have, your like an old woman)
They have successful children, your time is running out. ~~You need your job,~~ its all you have, they can all walk in + out of jobs anywhere.
You just have to face facts, your little Mr Average.
You cannot get away with calling people dogs, the others can but you just lack - ~~IT!~~
This morning was the first time I listened to you for ages + when the other ~~2 Dorks~~ did it, it was even more ~~PATHETIC.~~
People are getting fed up with you talking about your mum, your dad + his health, your sister + her kids, we don't want FAMILY FAVOURITES. Then we have to put up with sorting your computer out, that's just to let everyone know you have one, now it's your ~~first real property,~~ we don't want your life story.
You even slagged ████ off, why?
Dork 3 cannot count. I did not phone your show 7 times, it was 5 times actually + I gave my name and how could I go on air again, your rule is once a week + I had already been on once about the dog remark.

Cont..

Ian, except you wont have much longer + with a few
more letters like this you will be out, NO NEW
CONTRACT FOR YOU. Someone else will take over so
DORK, start looking about + you have that big
mortgage around your neck too – oh dear.
Now Ian, read this bit slowley so it sinks in, don't
bother giving it the big one IF you read this out on
air, because my radio will be OFF
If you do want an argument, my address is at the top
of this letter, so make an appointment with me, bring
someone with you + if I have time to fit 2 dorks in
my day for an argument, I will see you. OK, I don't
normally see dork's but I'll tell you all I wrote to
your face.

PS why does dork 3 put on more of a cockney accent,
is that to help or try and win some extra
callers???????

PPS There's just nothing to say About dork 2 because
he's just – dork 2, brain dead + Ian your were tops
brain dead and are out of your depth Ha Ha Ha –
PATHETIC

You sad little person

Collins,
Heard your show the other night, making sarcastic remarks about Manchester United. Tosser. Envy is a terrible thing.
I've noticed how you claim to be a Chelsea fan! Funny a few years back you didn't actually own up to this. Yet as soon as Chelsea started picking up a few trophys (as my Forrest supporting neighbour pointed out) we get all the "I'm a Chelsea fan bollocks"
And they call us united fans bandwagon jumpers. Fuck off you bastard. I hope you get injured in a car crash before the years out or get the boot.
Better still take a helicopter ride in a Matthew Harding special!

Female London United fan

WHO PAYS YOUR WAGES? — TONY BLAIR? ISN'T IT ILLEGAL TO BE PARTISAN ON ~~A~~ NATIONAL MATTER~~S~~? YOU APPEAR TO BE ON THE LABOUR PARTY PAYROLL..

Are you a lifelong supporter of the Tory party? We don't want your right wing crap. So go and preach in nazi fucking Germany. Please can you do us

Have you ever been afraid? Have you ever been afraid? Have you ever been Afraid?
Do you know what it feels like to write a letter knowing that the person who receives it will write it of as 'just another nutter?'
Do you know what it feels like to be the person sending it, knowing that you're not another nutter and that you will carry out everything you say?
That Mr C makes you very unsure and me very happy.
By the way, how's the car? Are you still driving the same one, the blue one?
I must have spent 3 weeks watching you going in and out of work. It's quite a sad little site, seeing you pull up in the car park and then get out with your little work bag to go and talk more shit for another night. Bet you didn't know I was there did you. Couldn't be there last Wednesday though, had to go shopping - wouldn't you like to know.
I'll probably be there all this week, but you won't see me anyway. Sometimes I'm around when you leave for work (Bet you didn't think I knew that either).
Your problem sir is working out when I am and when I'm not. That, as they, is something you will never know.
To be honest, you won't even see me coming. I'll be there when you least expect it. It might not even be on a day that you're working. Could be the weekend when you're out with that piece of blonde arm candy. But don't worry, what you won't see, you will feel. And yes, you will feel it. Very, very slowly, but you will feel it. The problem for you is how long you'll lay in your house with your throat cut before someone finds you. That could be days. Imagine that, you without your dignity just lying in your little house in your own insignificant blood and urine. Hope there's no one special in your life Ian. You'll make an awfully messy sight to discover after a few days.
By the way, enjoy your weekend. I'll be listening next week, but only for the first few days, obviously

Bye Bye

Chapter 9.

How to get into Radio

There's a genuine problem with radio talent in this country. The biggest scandal is that some of the real creative minds don't even work in the industry. It's a catastrophe. The reasons are arguably numerous, although for many, their story would be all too familiar: it's a closed shop, you have to know someone, they don't recognise talent. The list, sadly, goes on. In this section I will outline some of my own beliefs about entering the heady world of the wireless and illustrate how I see UK radio today. This section also includes what I hope are some useful tips and some valuable advice.

Over the last decade or so, radio in the UK has evolved into an industry almost unrecognisable from the one it set out to be. As more stations come on board and fewer companies become the collective owners, the emphasis has shifted. The market place is crowded and therefore competition is rife. This makes for exciting times and my cherished "may the best man win" philosophy is up and running like never before. Over the coming years we may well see a scenario where just two companies own all of independent radio. In turn, those companies may well be owned by the only two major TV companies, who in addition, may also have newspaper and Internet interests. In the USA this has gone even further with major utility corporations being at the helm of the country's biggest media. Whilst radio is getting bigger in terms of listener choice, everything is getting a whole lot smaller in terms of ownership. To those who own and run British radio, this is hardly revealing stuff: it's a forgone conclusion. Companies vying for domination of the dial have known for years that the future stability of any commercial radio company lies in multiple ownership and ideally, diversification.

There's a school of thought that business people simple don't understand creativity. In turn, it's argued that those on the creative side (on air) have no interest in how the bills are paid. To an extent, some of this is true, although it should perhaps be noted that the person who sign the cheques, by definition, pays others to manage and concern themselves with matters of creative output. Nobody, however, should be thinking about a career in radio without first knowing a little about the mechanics of the business side too. It's also important - in fact vital - to understand the new culture of UK commercial radio. I firmly believe that opportunities are missed, or not taken up, simply through a lack of understanding of the industry itself. There will be budding jocks and hosts reading this thinking, 'But I want to be the on air talent, not an accountant!' Fine, but if you really want to get ahead it pays to know what's going on. Rupert Murdoch and Ted Turner didn't get where they are today by not knowing what the hell was happening – everywhere. With radio being how it is today, it's only by having a full brief of how it works, that you can even begin to work out where you want to be within it.

Most wannabe radio presenters or DJs (and there's a big difference) still have the rosy view of simply wanting to be on the radio to entertain the masses and "make a difference". Ten years ago when half the bods that ran UK radio seemed to know sweet FA and the other half knew even less, this might have been the case. My own view is that the real talent that came from the "Golden Age" of radio often did so *in spite* of various programme bosses and not because of them. Sure, there were some good guys and we all know who they are etc. but there were also a lot of over-paid, under-worked rot and some highly questionable ideology that seemed to permeate every corner of the industry. Today, things have moved on (yes, we can still name those questionable areas and indeed the people, it isn't yet perfect – I could make a list). Radio stations are now very delicate animals and have to be managed and programmed accordingly.

Therefore, as the business side of the industry has shifted, the criteria for getting in has changed too. Things are now extremely different from the not too distant days of your happy, cosy Local FM station. Essentially the job description of the "average" DJ has changed beyond recognition and if you don't understand that, then you'd better get out now.

The last paragraph is perhaps specific to one area of the industry – independent local radio (ILR) which is where most people look to cut their teeth and begin their career. Generally speaking, most local commercial music radio is the same. Over the last few years, the local angle has been virtually eradicated (aside from news bulletins) and the philosophy has been to play song after song and hit after hit. If you were to drive from Lands End to John O'Groats, you could listen to dozens of local stations and be forgiven for thinking they were all the same one ("This is your more music station", "30 minutes of non-stop music", "Another 10 in a row", and most staggeringly, "While the others are talking, we're playing more great songs!" – strange, since none of the others are talking).

Here's the Paradox.

A large percentage of these "jukebox" radio stations are doing extremely well. Most dominate the dial within their transmission area and many have higher company profiles than other local leading brand names. In addition, because many are part of larger groups, they are able to diversify in the sales markets by offering advertisers not just a local coverage but also air time within the other stations in the group. Suddenly your favourite local radio station is able to market and sell on a larger regional and even national level.

Most radio companies now have their own "sales houses" enabling them to carefully, and brilliantly, tailor packages to the specific needs of the advertiser. On top of all of this, radio groups employ image makers, consultants and public relations departments to assist with the cosmetic side and to ensure that listeners and advertisers needs are met while tastes evolve and competition increases. In addition to any legally binding audience surveys, stations also pay out, at great expense, for their own independent "tracking" which can give handy (although sometimes grossly inaccurate) reports on the peaks and troughs of a stations performance. Tracking is also used as a tool to measure the attraction and performance of individual presenters as well as assessing the on-air success of competitions, jingle packages and station sound.

The reason these formats works is, in part, because they're all doing the same thing. Despite competition being as rife as it is, in an odd way it suits all to be churning out the same or similar formats. In many ways it's like price-fixing: if your choice of four local stations are all offering an almost identical product, it gives them all a chance for an identical success. This strategy, whilst a tad perverse, is, in the main, the lesser of two evils. An outsider will naturally argue that given this climate, there's a great opportunity for an individual station to shine above the others. On paper, this is true and nobody knows it more than the bosses themselves. The Programme Director (PD) could quite easily employ Shaggy McGinty, the hilarious off-the-wall breakfast jock but in doing so she risks dividing the audience. Dear old Shaggy may well double the reach on his first ever survey – great. The problem is, he's got to sustain that and better it, and then better it again.

For a radio station to show advertisers its success, it not only has to prove a healthy targeted demographic but also consistency within its audience levels. However bland you may think your local FM is, the chances are it boasts consistency in its audience reach. Whatever the accusations of banality which are levelled at these formats, they function on a low risk, maximum music, less talk ideology that actually works. In what other business would we suggest this kind of methodology is wrong?

By now, you should be getting a glimpse of the bigger picture. Local radio is a far cry from just being a cute and cuddly addition to the local community. It's big business, very big business. Essentially, programmers and Radio Groups don't need to take additional risks - why would you want to when your current format seems to be working fine?

Fortunately, there are now some chinks of light. You will have noticed that most local FM formats now boast a "personality" breakfast show. It's usually what's referred to as a Zoo format, meaning that the voice of more than one person is on air: the Travel Person, the News Reader, the Host and Co-Host are all there to provide a bit of craaazy early morning fun for the regional masses. This philosophy is now being extended to the late night shows, where many stations are now introducing a phone-in element and invariably opting for two presenters rather than one (a double header). The irony is that many of these stations once existed on the staple diet of their late night phone-in host.

When companies were bought out or merged with larger groups, many of the formats, particularly phone-in related, were frowned upon and deemed to be a distraction from the seriousness of a quality music station. An extremely high profile programme director recently said to me that they've now begun to realise that "something a bit different and phone based" actually works at night. Bingo! It took the guy this long to realise that? To be fair, I think this mentality only arose when the Big Boys came in to scoop up smaller stations and realised that the presentation teams were functioning virtually on a laissez-faire ticket. As I said above, some of these stations were working *in spite* of the management and not because of it. There was no proper music formula, no real identity, and no coherent on-air sound. This made for some rough and ready radio (nothing like hearing the DJ of one programme start his show with the same record that the last DJ had only just played!) and for many, those days were dynamite in terms of sheer, non-stop entertainment. In the grander scale however, many of those formats didn't allow for the growth and competition that the new market place would produce. Therefore, when the new bosses arrived, they needed (and rightly so) to take the reins. Management are strange old beasts and I never saw a new boss arrive anywhere and not change something. So it was out with the old and in with the new. As the years have moved on (and this is all still relatively new) many of the old ideas are beginning to return, sometimes re-packaged, but certainly on the way back. The difference is that now it's done as part and parcel of a structured business strategy.

So, in summary, what has happened is that UK radio has taken a leaf out of the American book: you go for a personality breakfast show and a personality late show and retain the jukebox music format for the remainder of the day. It's hard to argue against. Every survey that was ever done on music radio has shown that what people want from their "Much More Music Station" is, well, much more music. That said, we do have to be wary of surveys. I have a sneaking suspicion that many stations shell out hundreds of thousands of pounds just so that a survey company can simply tell them exactly what they want to hear. Station bosses often employ them simply to confirm what they *think* they already know. If you were set to coin in a few hundred grand from a large company you're hardly going to want to tell the boss that his entire ideology is wrong! At best, surveying should be treated with as much caution as BBC focus groups.

Contrary to popular belief, radio bosses do want talent. They do want originality and they are on the lookout for performance-enhancing ideas. What they don't want is anything that's going to detract from a product that they know works. It might be safe, it might not be highly creative, but it works. Why would a multi-million pound organisation want to jeopardise that? It's not that this format is the best, it's just the best they've come across *so far*.

You may think I'm biased. I work in speech based formats that give room for creativity and space for ideas. I do feel passionately about "creative radio" and therefore I have an interest and an inherent belief that UK music radio could still be better. Of course music stations (which sadly in the UK are generally chart music stations – apart from when they spin that token oldie from the "Classic Files") should be playing lots of music, but they could also be doing a whole lot more too. Everything about British media today is risk free and whilst the commercial arguments for that are strong, they're not exclusive.

When I first started in local Music Radio, I was based at Invicta FM in Kent. Within our listening range there was on offshore pirate station called Laser 558. It was mainly hosted by Americans and boasted that you were "Never More Than a Minute Away From Music" - it was your regular ten-records-in-a-row type station. I remember our head of music saying to me that within a few years, conventional legal stations in mainland UK will be doing the same thing. This was just 8 years ago. He was right, and what seemed unthinkable has not only happened but now constitutes the norm. I believe that under the circumstances, music station bosses currently have it about 70% right, but as with the Laser 558 example, it's only a matter of time before a new format breaks through, and proves successful. When it does, like baby lambs, the other stations will follow.

The problem for you is that you're not looking for a career in radio just so you can spin ten records in a row and read the weather forecast every half an hour. You want to entertain, you want to be noticed – doesn't everyone? Chances are, you aspire to certain high profile radio individuals who've made their mark by doing everything that these music stations don't do. You probably have ideas, formats and styles that you want to implement NOW. All this is fine and you should never think you're on a hiding to nothing just because you can't see an initial way in for your particular approach. You just have to play the game. Once you're in, then you can begin experimenting. I know that at least one person will be reading this chapter and be thinking it is irrelevant to them. Perhaps it is, but as I said at the beginning, it is crucial to know and understand the culture of the industry before you can decide where you want to be and how you're going to play it.

So What's the Quickest Way in?

Like any industry, there's no set route. There is however, a "most taken" route.
There's hardly anyone I've worked with who didn't at some point work for nothing in order to get into radio. When you mention work experience people often think of a few weeks in a radio station as part of an educational course. It doesn't have to be that way. For whatever reason, this simplest of routes appears to many, unattainable. Perhaps it's the age-old problem of believing someone else will get there before you or maybe a case of just having too little faith in yourself. There are a few things to remember here. Most radio stations don't have a separate department that deals specifically with work experience applications. It isn't uncommon for applicants' letters to be sent between departments so many times, they eventually find their way in to the bin. With this in mind, try sending your letters to more than one person. Send them to editors, producers, the presenters themselves. Follow those letters up with a phone call or an email. If you don't hear anything after a while then write again and if you feel you're having no success, change your approach. Find another way of phrasing your letter and try sending it to other stations to see if you get a different answer. It is vital that you make sure you are actually offering something other than your ability to make the tea. It's also important to create a balance between healthy enthusiasm and becoming a pain in the butt.

Much of being taken on is about timing. You could write to a producer one week and she may tell you there's nothing doing. The next week she might need some tapes filed or some music timed and could have done with the extra help. Therefore when applying for experience, suggest certain areas in which you may be of use. Don't just ask for a week sitting in the studio, give some ideas of what you can offer. Believe me, there's not a person in radio who couldn't do with an extra pair of hands - it's your job to convince them that you're that pair of hands. Whenever I've taken on work experience people, I've nearly always chosen those whose applications stood out. Whether it was because of what they specifically offered, their previous experience or just natural enthusiasm, nearly everyone who gets a gig, gets it because their initial correspondence was that bit different.

Once you're in, you're in (providing you don't monumentally screw things up). What might start out as one week in radio, could easily end up being two weeks. If you've made an impact you may get asked to come back on a semi regular basis, or even be told to show up whenever you feel you can spare the time. I'm a firm believer that immersing yourself in an environment is paramount to success.

You may be working for nothing but you'll be experiencing the day-to-day feel of how a broadcasting company works. You'll begin to know the faces and develop the required working practises without having to think twice. Soaking-in a working atmosphere is to my mind imperative to both your understanding of the industry and your future prospects within it. You may be working for free - or on occasions for a pittance - but the point is, you'll be living, breathing, and being mentally stimulated by that world. Eventually, your hard work and persistence, as well as that frame of mind, will pay dividends. Initially you may be offered just the odd shift or perhaps some regular but part-time work. If you shine and prove reliable, believe me, that work will eventually become more permanent. You have no idea how many times, to this day, I hear producers and programmers desperate for people to fill a shift. I've seen bosses have to beg and cut deals with existing staff members to get them out of a hole purely because they couldn't find anyone else to cover the gig. If you tell that to some of the million people out there trying to get into the industry in the first place, they'd never believe you. The work is there and work experience is the key. It might not always be easy and it does take persistence and hard work, and you do have to be genuinely willing to learn, but the opportunities, quite seriously, are there.

As I sit and write these words I know of at least 3 national radio stations that at some level can't find staff for this coming weekend – how bad is that? You may think I'm being simplistic with all of this. Have I really just given a whole bunch of people the key to that door called radio in just a few short paragraphs? Well, yes. Forget expensive media seminars for the moment (they do have a place) or ten thousand page books by some Joe who hasn't worked in the media for three decades, I'm talking from the inside here. I feel passionately that really talented people, many of whom have just completed superb media degrees, are missing out for no other reason than the age-old belief that radio is a closed shop. I may be telling you what you already know. The point is that many of you will not yet have bothered, for whatever reason, to put a plan in to action.

Remember to list your goals. Make a logged note of what you want to do, where you want to go, why you want to be there and when you want to achieve it by. Don't limit your ambitions and aims, keep that list open and add to it or change it as necessary. Remember, this is your world and you've a right to be anywhere on it at any time you wish. Listing your plans is vital.

I'm aware that some of you will have no intention of going into local music radio. Many will want to work in speech formats, might be looking at local BBC, or at sports departments, or at news and current affairs. I chose to base the bulk of this chapter on local music radio because that's where 90% will be looking to start. However, most of the guidelines and tips below will apply no matter which area you're looking to begin or continue your career.

TIPS FOR GETTING IN

- Always record a demo at a professional studio. Quality makes the difference and it'll be well worth the money. Package your demo properly. Don't just grab an old supermarket cassette tape and stick your phone number on the side in marker pen. Make it look professional. It could be your only chance. Try not to make the demo last more than 5 minutes. Programme managers haven't got enough time to be listening to hours of audition tapes.

- If you're just making a standard DJ demo tape, be original - but don't try anything too complicated. Managers will hear what they want to hear from your voice and style itself. Anything else – features & ideas – are useful but merely cosmetic.

- If you're making a demo for music-based formats it's imperative that you cut out the main chunk of the songs. The demo just needs the intro and outro of each track. You wouldn't believe how many people don't do that and lose out.

- Avoid using "listings" on your demo. It's the easiest thing in the world to read out a list of "Top albums" or "Best chat up lines" etc. Don't do it. It's lazy, predictable and unimaginative.

- A programme manager wants to hear what she might hear on air - travel, weather etc. It might be predictable but simplicity is always the best approach. Being simplistic doesn't mean that you can't be imaginative. Include some light and shade as well as topicality.

- Don't be afraid to buck convention. There's a school of thought that a demo is a demo, end of story. It might be that you want to submit an idea or package rather than a full audition tape. This is fine. There's nothing wrong with sending specific ideas or features – it's often more applicable if you're applying for producer or production roles, although even as a DJ, it can be an easier way in.

- Know the station you're applying to. Be familiar with its format, its on-air line up, its features and competitions. Remember, the boss isn't looking to do you a great favour by giving you the gig, she's looking to see what you can do for her. Make sure your ideas and suggestions are compatible with the output of the station and the on-air sound. Look to complement a format as opposed to just adding to it.

- Be familiar with the business side of the station. Know who the Chairman is, the MD and the programme management team. Familiarise yourself with other stations within the company and don't be afraid to show your knowledge in an interview.

- Think simplicity. If submitting ideas, don't write a book - make your case in bullet points and keep pages to a minimum. Bosses are busy people who want an idea to jump at them, not to have to search it out in a novel.

- Don't think conspiracy. Radio is not a closed shop. They want good people and good ideas. Again, it's about offering the right thing to the right station. Many mistakes are made by sending good tapes to the wrong people or station.

- Send your applications, ideas and tapes to more than one person. PD's are inundated with tapes, so why not try sending your packages to individual presenters and producers.

- As I outlined above, always try for work experience. It's the most common way in. Don't just write to Management, write to individual presenters and producers too. Keep following up the letters if need be and don't be concerned if it takes a while for a reply. Never offer to make the tea, it's the most obvious and overused line there is. I await the day when someone writes to me and says "I'll do anything except make the tea!"

- Never be afraid of unpaid work. It sounds tough but most people in radio did it at some point. It isn't exploitation, it's experience that you can't get anywhere else.

- Know the Radio Authority rules and regulations. Be particularly aware of libel laws and areas involving defamation.

- Write to the Radio Authority and obtain as much information on ILR as you can. There's a booklet available that lists all ILR stations in the UK. You can also get details of new stations starting up and information about licence applications. All very useful.

- Play the game. If a station is not your ideal cup of tea, don't worry. You can always get more experimental once you have your foot in the door. A Programme manager may well be reluctant to run with a particular idea at application level but could be open to that suggestion once that person is in the door. Don't lose out just because everything doesn't appear to be 100% "you" to start with. As I said above, there's nothing wrong with bucking convention and if the situation is right that should be encouraged, just be realistic about the parameters you are doing it within.

- Be yourself. It sounds so obvious but it's still the most important piece of advice. You can have all the jingles and sound effects in the world (and used correctly they can be great) but nothing will hide you, the voice. It's YOU they want to hear, nothing else.

CREATURE FACT
At least 10 people who have had work experience with Ian Collins & the Creatures of the Night have now moved into professional Radio and TV. Positions include presentation, producing, technical production and journalism.
You see, it does work!

Useful Names and Numbers

The Radio Authority

For anyone serious about working in the radio industry from management to production the Radio Authority is a useful place to know. In some ways it is like the Government of the commercial airwaves - essential to understanding the current climate.

Radio Authority
Holbrook House
14 Great Queen Street
Holborn
London
WC2B 5DG
Switchboard (9:00 am - 6:00 pm): +44 (0) 20 7430 2724
Fax: +44 (0) 20 7405 7062
Internet: http://www.radioauthority.org.uk
Email: reception@radioauthority.org.uk

DCMS (Department for Culture, Media and Sport)

The Department for Culture, Media and Sport is responsible for Government policies on broadcasting, including radio. The Secretary of State for Culture, Media and Sport appoints the Members of the Radio Authority.

2-4 Cockspur Street, London SW1Y 5DH
Tel: 0171 211 6200 Fax: 0171 211 6032
Internet: http://www.culture.gov.uk

Radio Joint Audience Research Ltd (RAJAR)

RAJAR is a company specifically established to manage the UK's agreed system of radio audience measurement. It is jointly owned by the CRCA (on behalf of commercial radio companies) and by the BBC.

Gainsborough House, 81 Oxford Street, London W1D 2EU
Tel: 020 7903 5350 Fax: 020 7903 5351
e-mail: info@rajar.co.uk
Internet: http://www.rajar.co.uk

Student Radio Association

The Student Radio Association is the representative body for student radio in the UK. Run by an elected committee of volunteers drawn from its 40 member stations, the SRA holds an annual conference and organises the Radio 1 Student Radio Awards.

C/O The Radio Academy, 5 Market Place, London W1N 7AH
Tel: 0171 255 2010 Fax: 0171 255 2029
e-mail: sra-exec@studentradio.org.uk
Internet: http://www.studentradio.org.uk

The Radio Magazine

Specialist magazine with all the industry gossip as well as job vacancies – order it now. An extremely useful publication if you want to know what's happening on a regular basis.

Internet: http://www.theradiomagazine.co.uk

The Media Guardian

Comes out every Monday as a supplement to the main newspaper. Many of the big broadcasters in all areas of the media advertise vacancies here. There is also a Saturday addition. There's hardly a soul in the radio industry who doesn't buy it each week.

Stage and Television Newspaper

You might have to order this from your newsagents. This weekly publication isn't exactly a focus for radio although from time to time vacancies may appear in it. It is however a useful paper for keeping abreast of other aspects of the industry.

The Writers Handbook

Again, not a dedicated radio manual, but a useful book for addresses and phone numbers of various media related organisations. You'll find a copy in most book stores.

So there you go kids, one radio book complete. Putting this thing together took more time than I had originally anticipated. That said, I loved every bit of it. For those who listen to the show regularly, I trust this book proved to be an insight. For those who picked this up by chance, I hope, if nothing else, you found it different. Those of you who bought the book who want to crack it in the radio industry itself, I trust it proved and continues to prove useful. And remember, if you thought this book was odd, you should hear the CD.

...And Finally

BONUS CREATURE FACT

Since Ian and the team have worked together many things have happened in their private lives.....

One got married, one became a parent, 3 got engaged, 3 split from their long terms partners, one was mugged (twice), all have moved house, 3 lost a parent, one had a fling with a well known personality, 2 nearly quit just minutes before a show, one was mistakenly fired and then reinstated and 1 won a tad more than £1000 on the lottery. Now you've just got to figure out what happened to whom.

YOU'VE READ THE BOOK NOW
HEAR THE CD

Over an hour of top quality cuts from the Collins archives, containing new material *never* before heard on air.

STRICTLY LIMITED EDITION

- *I've Stolen Ya Red Top Missus* – this was banned from the radio!

- *Icons Corner with Brian Cant, Johnny Morris, Tony Hart and Peter Cushing*

- *Out-takes – never aired before (only for the broad-minded of course)*

- *The impossible caller – Ian nearly resigned after this call!*

- *The manic montage*

- *Archive Gold*

...*And heaps more*

"A must for every radio fan on the planet"

This CD is NOT available in any shops and can only be bought from the same address as you purchased this book or by visiting the web site
WWW.THERADIOBOOK.COM

Because you've already purchased this book, you're entitled to a full £4 discount (normal price £12). This one off offer is available for just £8 ($16 USA) and that's inclusive of all postage, packing and handling. Please make your cheques/postal orders payable to THE RADIO BOOK
NO CREDIT CARDS

THIS OFFER IS STRICTLY ON A FIRST COME, FIRST SERVED BASIS

This offer is NOT in conjunction with any radio station. Please allow 28 days for delivery

WWW.VOICEOFTHECOMMONMAN.COM

"THE GREATEST RADIO WEB SITE ON THE NET"

If you haven't yet been to the Creature web site then shame on you. The fantastic Andy kicked all this off, ably assisted by a top team of web experts. So don't dilly-dally, get in there a bit lively and have a gander – muppets

- *More Creature info*
- *Film Section*
- *Book at Bog time*
- *Chat Room*
- *Message board*
- *Freaks Gallery*
- *More photos*

"YOU'LL BE HARD PUSHED TO FIND A RADIO WEB SITE QUITE AS BUSY AND AS HOT AS THIS MOTHER"

Well, go on then, log on and surf!

WWW.VOICEOFTHECOMMONMAN.COM